科技英语丛书

化学专业英语
English for Chemistry

缪煜清　编著

中国科学技术大学出版社

内 容 简 介

本书不是简单地阅读化学相关的文字,而是在传授一种思维和学习方法,其内容分为三个模块:基于分析方法的词汇学习、以基础化学词汇为主的短文学习、学科领域的范文参考。它不是对整篇文章进行学习,而是以单词、短语、短句、短文为主,有效地避免冗长乏味的感觉。通过对词汇的溯源、比较和关联,建立一种基于分析的词汇学习方法,这种方法追本溯源、由表及里、由此及彼、由点及面、层层递进、彼此相连,有助于建立起牢固的网格状词汇体系。

本书可作为化学及其相关专业的本科生或研究生教材,也可作为本科生考研用书,有助于在短时间内迅速提高化学专业英语水平。

图书在版编目(CIP)数据

化学专业英语/缪煜清编著. —合肥:中国科学技术大学出版社,2015.8(2019.4重印)

ISBN 978-7-312-03721-4

Ⅰ.化… Ⅱ.缪… Ⅲ.化学—英语—高等学校—教材 Ⅳ.H31

中国版本图书馆 CIP 数据核字(2015)第 140022 号

出版	中国科学技术大学出版社 安徽省合肥市金寨路 96 号,230026 http://press.ustc.edu.cn
印刷	安徽省瑞隆印务有限公司
发行	中国科学技术大学出版社
经销	全国新华书店
开本	710 mm×960 mm 1/16
印张	11.75
字数	236 千
版次	2015 年 8 月第 1 版
印次	2019 年 4 月第 2 次印刷
定价	28.00 元

前　言

　　无论是对本科生还是研究生，专业英语的学习都非常重要，它能使学生及时掌握本学科领域的最新科技进展，培养其全球化视野，也有助于其今后承担科学研究和科技开发任务或者进一步求学深造。本人多年来承担本科生化学专业英语的教学工作，也带领研究生在化学相关领域开展学术研究。在此过程中，发现大部分学生对化学专业英语有畏难情绪，普遍认为化学专业英语枯燥难学。其实化学专业英语的难度主要是在词汇，因为化学专业英语的语法通常比较简单，但词汇却较为晦涩难懂，因为很多词汇平时并不多见，而且化学领域经常出现组合词，又长又难记。

　　笔者认为，化学专业英语难学的根本原因在于我们仅仅把它当作一门工具来学习，剥离其内涵的学习必然是枯燥的。实际上，化学并非孤立于这个世界，它深深植根于整个科学体系，它也伴随着语言、文化、文明的发展而发展。很多化学词汇的背后有丰富的人文背景，比如与一些化学元素的名称和希腊神话或者罗马神话相关。许多化学词汇实际上和我们平时所熟知的单词同源。词汇看起来千变万化，仔细分析却又彼此关联，甚至也体现出一定的哲学思想。这本书是一个有益的尝试，尝试结合文化思考从词汇分析的角度来学习化学专业英语。

　　本书写作主要以 Kenneth W Whitten 等人编著的教材 *Chemistry* (*Eighth Edition*) 中的内容为范例进行讲解；阅读参考资料引自维基百科(Wikipedia)。词汇分析的理论依据参见拙著《巧妙学单词——从象形到读音》(中国科学技术大学出版社，2015)。其他未能一一列举，在此一并表示感谢！

缪煜清

2015 年 3 月

目 录

前言	···	(i)
1	学习方法 ···	(1)
2	化学之学 ···	(2)
3	化学分支 ···	(5)
4	词义辨证 ···	(7)
5	数字顺序 ···	(10)
6	程度词汇 ···	(18)
7	位置词汇 ···	(21)
8	词汇分析 ···	(24)
9	阿拉伯语中的化学词汇 ···························	(27)
10	炼金术七金属 ·····································	(28)
11	元素命名 ···	(32)
12	常用元素词根 ·····································	(35)
13	无机化学命名 ·····································	(42)
14	有机化学命名 ·····································	(46)
15	化学基础 ···	(53)
16	化学式与组成 ·····································	(58)
17	化学反应 ···	(61)
18	原子结构 ···	(67)
19	元素周期律 ·······································	(72)
20	化学键 ··	(75)
21	价键理论 ···	(78)
22	气体动力学分子理论 ·····························	(81)
23	化学热力学 ·······································	(84)
24	化学动力学 ·······································	(88)
25	气体、液体和固体 ································	(90)
26	分散体系 ···	(94)
27	水溶液与酸碱盐 ··································	(97)

28 电化学 ……………………………………………………… (101)
29 大型仪器 …………………………………………………… (104)
30 常用化学仪器装置 ………………………………………… (108)
31 化学试剂 …………………………………………………… (111)
32 化学论文 …………………………………………………… (114)
33 化学会议 …………………………………………………… (119)
34 无机化学* ………………………………………………… (124)
35 分析化学* ………………………………………………… (132)
36 有机化学* ………………………………………………… (142)
37 物理化学* ………………………………………………… (152)
38 纳米技术* ………………………………………………… (156)
39 材料科学* ………………………………………………… (173)

* 阅读参考资料。

1　学习方法

英语难学,专业英语更难学,化学专业英语更是难上加难。这是很多学生对化学专业英语的印象。然而,只要掌握了方法,学习化学专业英语就会事半功倍,甚至会从中感受到学习的乐趣,学习化学专业英语也有助于英语水平的提升。

1. 溯源式学习

许多单词或者词根可以追溯其词源,通过源头可以发现很多单词产生、变化、发展的过程,也会了解很多单词的同源性。

2. 发散式学习

由表及里、由此及彼、由点及面、层层递进,建立引申式、发散式学习方法。

3. 关联式学习

对词汇之间的相似性、相异性、相关性、同源性进行比较,可以实现相类词群的学习。

通过以上词汇的学习方法,彼此相连,学一个掌握一群,形成根深叶茂、牢固坚实的网格状词汇体系,在头脑中建立根深蒂固的记忆。

2 化学之学

化学的英文是 chemistry,有人风趣地称之为 Chem-is-try,意思是说"化学就是试验"。

实际上化学是从古代的炼金术发展而来的,chemistry 来自阿拉伯词汇 alchemy,炼金术的意思。更古老的词源甚至可以追溯到古埃及词汇 Khemia,"黑化"的意思,是炼金术的第一个步骤。

说到化学 chemistry,我们可以联想到数学 mathematics、生物学 biology、物理学 physics、地理学 geography 等词汇。它们都是"……学",却有着完全不同的构词。实际上,在英语中表示"……学"的词汇有很多:

1. -stry

表示集合名词。
dentistry 牙医学、forestry 林学
industry 工业、ancestry 祖先

2. -ics

表示"科学或学科",原意为"与……相关的专门研究"。
physics 物理学、acoustics 声学、dynamics 动力学 、economics 经济学、arithmetic 算术、logics 逻辑学、analytics 分析学、mechanics 力学
aerobics 有氧健身法
basics 基本原理、classics 名著、典范

3. -ology

表示"知识、科学的分支"。该词源与 logic 有关,有"话语、逻辑、理性、真理"等含义。
biology 生物学、crystallology 晶体学、enzymology 酶学、petrology 岩石学、demology 人口学、geology 地质学

4．-graphy

表示与"书写、画图、绘图、测量"相关的技艺或研究。

来自古希腊词汇 graphe，意为"写、画"。graphite 石墨/黑铅、graph 图/图表显然和这个词源有关。

cartography 制图学、oceanography 海洋学、geography 地理学
crystallography 晶体学、demography 人口统计学
calligraphy 书法、biography 自传

5．-scopy

来自希腊词源 skopein，原意为"看、观察、检察"等含义。由此衍生出与"观察、光"等相关的技术。

scopy 镜检/检查法/观察
scope 眼界/审视/仔细研究
microscopy 显微术/显微检查法、spectroscopy 光谱学、radioscopy 放射性检测法

6．-sophy

来自希腊词源 sophia，表示"智慧"。
欧美常用女子名 Sophia，译为索菲亚或者苏菲，就是智慧的意思了。
philosophy 哲学、theosophy 通神学

7．-metry

来自古希腊词根-metros，表示"测量"，与长度单位 meter"米"同源，由此衍生出"测量、仪表"及其相关的技术或学科。

stoichiometry 化学计量学、amperometry 电流测定法、potentiometry 电位分析法、geometry 几何学、conductivity meter 电导仪、pH meter pH 计

8．化学专业英语

专业英语可以表示为：Special English、Specialized English、Scientific English、Technical English、English for the Professionals、English for Special Purposes……

相应地，化学专业英语可以表示为：

English in Chemistry
English on Chemistry
Professional English on Chemistry
English for Chemistry
English for Specific Purposes: Chemistry
可以总结为:
General/Professional/Technical/Academic/ Scientific English for/in/on Chemistry
当然,仔细推敲会发现其中微妙的差异。

3 化学分支

化学历来以四大化学为主干,从中派生出很多分支。

1. 四大化学

organic chemistry 有机化学、inorganic chemistry 无机化学、analytical chemistry 分析化学、physical chemistry 物理化学

> organic 有机的/系统的/器官的、organ 器官/机构/元件
> organize 组织、self-organization/self-assembly 自组织/自组装
> self-organized monolayer/self-assembled monolayer 自组装单层

> analytical 分析的、analyst 分析家/化验员、analyte 分析物
> analysis 分析/分解,其中-lysis 来自古希腊词汇,源头甚至可以追溯到古印欧语,表示分解、散开等含义,相关词汇如:
> lysis 溶解/融化/裂解、hydrolysis 水解、electrolysis 电解、pyrolysis 热解、glycolysis 糖酵解
> lose 失去/错过、loose 松散/释放
> 相似词汇还有 solve,表示解决、解答之意。该词汇同样来自古印欧语词根 se-lu 或者 se-leu,其中-lu-/leu 即为分解、分散、散开之意。
> dissolve 使溶解
> 由此衍生的词还有 solution 溶液,意味着一种溶质在溶剂中的分散。
> resolution 解析度/精度/分辨率

2. 常见化学分支学科

applied chemistry 应用化学、biological chemistry 生物化学、colloid chemistry 胶体化学、coordination chemistry 配位化学、crystal chemistry 晶体化学、electroanalytical chemistry 电分析化学、general chemistry 普通化学、structural chemistry 结构化学

3. 其他化学分支学科

agricultural chemistry 农艺化学、archaeological chemistry 考古化学、bioinorganic chemistry 生物无机化学、biomimetic chemistry 仿生化学、biophysical chemistry 生物物理化学、computational quantum chemistry 计算量子化学、engineering chemistry 工程化学、food chemistry 食品化学、judicial chemistry 法医化学、forest chemistry 森林化学、free-redical chemistry 自由基化学、geological chemistry 地质化学、heterocyclic chemistry 杂环化学、high polymer chemistry 高分子化学、histological chemistry 组织化学、hygienic chemistry 卫生化学、isotope chemistry 同位素化学、laser chemistry 激光化学、magneto chemistry 磁化学、marine physical chemistry 海洋物理化学、metabolic chemistry 代谢化学、metallurgical chemistry 冶金化学、mineralogical chemistry 矿物化学、nuclear chemistry 核化学、organometallic chemistry 有机金属化学、pathological chemistry 病理化学、petroleum chemistry 石油化学、physical chemistry 物理化学、physiological chemistry 生理化学、theoretical chemistry 理论化学、quantum chemistry 量子化学、radiological chemistry 放射化学、sanitary chemistry 卫生化学、soil chemistry 土壤化学、space chemistry 立体化学、toxicological chemistry 毒物化学、tracer chemistry 示踪化学

4 词义辨证

1. 同和异

iso-同：isotope 同位素、isoelectric point 等电点、isotherm 等温线

iso-异：isomer 异构体、isooctane 异辛烷、isolate 分离

比较上面两段文字会发现一个有趣的现象，就是 iso-词根有时翻译为"同"，有时则翻译为"异"，那么这是怎么一回事呢？仔细思考，其实也不难理解：

同位素是指具有相同质子数、不同中子数或同一元素的不同核素互为同位素，这里 isotope 强调的彼此之间共同的部分——"具有相同质子数"，因此称之为同位素。

异构体是指具有相同化学式，不同结构的化合物，这里 isomer 异构体强调的是彼此不同的地方——"结构不同"。

所以对同位素而言，它们尽管具有不同中子数，但却有相同质子数；对异构体而言，它们尽管具有相同化学式，但却有不同结构。正所谓"同中有异、异中有同，彼此相依，共同存在"，正如老子道德经所言：

"故有无相生，难易相成，长短相形，高下相倾，音声相和，前后相随。"

看来东西方思维也存在相似之处。

allotr-异：allotrope 同素异形体、allotriploid 异源三倍体、allotriomorphic 异形的、allotriolith 异质结石

说到同和异，还有一对词根也常用来表示同和异：

homo-同：homo 相同/人属、homogeneity 同种/均匀性、homogeneous reaction 均相反应

heter-异：heterogeneity 异质性、heterodimer 异二聚体、heterocyclic 杂环的、heterogeneous reaction 异相反应、heterosexual 异性的

normal-/n-正：n-propane 正丙烷、normal 正常/常规/标准

iso-异：isobutane 异丁烷

ortho-正/直：orthosilicic acid 原硅酸

meta-偏：metasilicic acid 偏硅酸

2. 一和多

uni-个体的：unit 单位、unicellular 单细胞的、unicorn 独角兽、unicycle 独轮车、unlateral 单边的、unique 独特的

uni-整体的：universal 普遍的/一致的、universe 宇宙/世界/万物、university 综合性大学、ubiquitous 无处不在的、unify 统一

比较上面两段词汇，发现 uni-词根在构词中既有个体的意思，又有整体的意思。这体现了个体与整体的统一：单位与其他单位相比是一个个体，但是单位又是组成自身的许多个体的集合；单细胞是一个个体，但它是无数成分所构成的一个整体；宇宙是一个整体，但它是由世界上的每一个成分所组成的；统一是把很多个体整合为一个整体……

类似的词根还有 per-每、ple/-ple/-ble 倍/多：

表示一个、单个的有：per 每次/每个、per cent/percent 百分比、period 一段时间/句号。

表示两个的有：pair 一对。

表示倍或者多的有：ple/-ple/-ble 倍、double 双倍、multiple 多倍的、complex 复杂的、plenty 满的、complete 完全的、aplenty 大量、ample 广大的、amplify 放大、triple 三倍的、duple 二倍的、duplicate 复制、plenary 全体出席的、plenitude 充分、plentiful 丰富的、plenum 全体会议。

3. 两性与爱恨亲疏

ampho-两：amphoteric 酸碱两性的、amphoteric ion 两性离子、ampholite 两性电解质、amphotericin 两性霉素、amphoteric emulsifier 两性乳化剂

图 4.1

ampho-词根来自 amphora，双耳瓶之意。

ambi-与 amphi-同源，表示周围、两边之意：

ambi-两/周围：ambiguous 模棱两可的、ambient 周围/两边、ambivalent 矛盾的

amphi-两：amphipathic/amphiphilic 两亲性的、amphibious 两栖的

这里 amphipathic/amphiphilic 两亲性的，表示的是既亲水又亲油的两种特性。

再看下面这两组词汇：

-phil-亲/爱：hydrophilic 亲水的/吸湿的、Philip 菲利普、philolosophy 哲学、

nucleophile 亲核试剂、lipophilic 亲脂的

-phob-疏/惧：hydrophobic 疏水的、phobe/phobia 恐惧

前者来自希腊词-philia 表示爱、亲、吸引的意思，后者来自-phobia 表示恐惧、害怕之意。

所以欧美常用人名 Philip 菲利普来自希腊文 Philippos，由 philo(爱)＋hippos(马)构成，爱马人的意思。

这里提出一个问题，为什么数学、物理、化学等学科的博士学位称之为 PhD(Doctor of Philosophy 哲学博士)？

philosophy 哲学，这里 philo-表示爱，-sophy 表示智慧，哲学就是爱智慧的意思，是自然知识和社会知识的概括和总结，后来也指除医学、法律、神学外的所有自然学科，因此数学、物理、化学等学科的博士学位仍然称之为 PhD 哲学博士。

5 数字顺序

在化学词汇中涉及很多与数字、数量、顺序相关的表达,而且同一个数字有几种表达方式,表 5.1 中可以发现它们之间的关系。

表 5.1

数字		基团		月份		其他	
zero	0					nil-	
one	1	methyl-	甲基	Jan.	一月	un(i)-/mon-/mono-	单
two	2	ethyl-	乙基	Feb.	二月	b(i)-/di-/deu-/do-/du-/dou-/amphi-/ambi-/twi-	二/双/重
three	3	propyl-	丙基	Mar.	三月	tr(i)-/ter-	三
four	4	butyl-	丁基	Apr.	四月	buty-/qua-/tetra-	四
five	5	amyl- pentyl- quintenyl-	戊基	May	五月	penta-/quin-	五
six	6	hexyl-	己基	Jun.	六月	hex-/hexa-	六
seven	7	heptyl-	庚基	Jul.	七月	hepta-/sept-	七
eight	8	octyl-	辛基	Aug.	八月	oct-/octa-	八
nine	9	nonyl-	壬基	Sept.	九月	nona-/nov-	九
ten	10	decyl-	癸基	Oct.	十月	dec-	十
				Nov.	十一月		
				Dec.	十二月		

1. 零相关词汇

零相关词汇通常用 zero 和 nil-表示,其中 nil-与否定词 no 相关,表示无。

no-无/零:no 没有、none 没有、nought 零、nonsense 废话

nil-无/零分:nil 无/零分、nill 不想/不愿、nilpotent 幂零

nu-零/无效的:null 零/无效的、nude 裸体的/无效的

2. 一相关词汇

one 一、a/an 一个

mono-单/一：monomer 单体、monocrystal 单晶、monochrome 单色的、mononuclear 单核的、monoxide 一氧化物、monologue 独白、monopoly 垄断

mon-单/一：monatomic 单原子的、monad 单细胞生物

> monday 星期一，其前缀 mon-不是表示"一"，而是表示"月亮"，该词根来自 moon，所以星期一也有月曜日的说法。

uni-单/一：uniaxial 单轴晶体、unit 个体、unique 唯一的
methyl 甲基、methylcellulose 甲基纤维素、methylamine 甲胺

3. 二相关词汇

ambi-两：ambiguous 模棱两可的、ambivalent 两性人/矛盾的

ampho-两：amphoteric 酸碱两性的、amphoteric ion 两性离子、ampholite 两性电解质、amphotericin 两性霉素、amphoteric emulsifier 两性乳化剂

amphi-两：amphipathic/amphiphilic 两亲性的、amphibious 两栖的

twi-二：twin 双胞胎、twice 两倍

tween80 是一种非离子活性剂，tween 表示在两者之间，在……中间。

马克·吐温的名字 Mark Twain，后者也表示"二"。

ethyl 乙基、ethylene 乙烯、ethylbenzene 乙苯

acetyl 乙酰基、acetate 乙酸、acetylene 乙炔

acetone 丙酮，这个单词是一个例外，因为最初发现它是乙酸 acetic acid 的衍生物。

bi-二：binoculars 双筒望远镜、bicycle 自行车

bicarbonate/dicarbonate 重碳酸盐、sodium bicarbonate 碳酸氢钠

碳酸氢钠英文 sodium bicarbonate 中 bi-词根表示二，要从二元含氧酸的正盐和酸式盐的关系说起，当碳酸和氢氧化钠发生中和反应时：

$$H_2CO_3 + 2NaOH = Na_2CO_3 + H_2O$$

当继续加入碳酸时，则生成碳酸氢钠：

$$2H_2CO_3 + 2NaOH = 2NaHCO_3 + 2H_2O$$

从中我们可以看出第二个反应碳酸的量是第一个反应的两倍，所以生成的盐就是酸式盐，是加了两倍的酸中和碱形成的盐，所以有"重"的意思。

bind 捆绑，有两者结合之意，派生出 bond 联系/价键，如 covalent bond 共价键、ionic bond 离子键。

combine 组合、联合，由 com-和 bi-组合而成，也是两者结合的意思。

> conjugate 共轭/结合、conjunction 连接/结合
> 其中-juga-和-junct-都是 yoke 的变体，yoke 表示牛轭，原意是把两头牛连在一起，有连接之义。
> 梵语中 yoga 瑜伽一词也来自 yoke，其梵语词根为 yuj-，通常解释为 to control 控制、to yoke 连接、to unite 联合。瑜伽就是把人的注意力集中起来加以引导、运用和实施，将身体和心灵的所有力量与神结合，达到天人合一的境界。

di-二：carbon dioxide 二氧化碳、dichloromethane 二氯甲烷、disulfide bond 二硫键、dilemma 进退两难、divide 分开

重铬酸钾英文 potassium dichromate 中含有 di-词根，是因为重铬酸 $H_2Cr_2O_7$ 是两个 H_2CrO_4 缩合而来。

deu-二：deuteroxide 重氢、deuce 两点

dou-二：double bond 双键、doubt 怀疑

du-二：dual 双的、duplicate 两倍的、dualism 二元论、duel 决斗

di-、deu-、du-、teu-与 two 应属同源。

与 di-类似，dis-也有一拍两散、分离、分别的意思，仔细思考，下列许多词汇均有潜在的"二"，表示两者之间的关系：

different/distinct 不同的、distinguish 区别、dispute 辩论、distribution 分发、discuss 讨论

4. 三相关词汇

propyl 丙基、propylene 丙烯、propane 丙烷

tri-三：trioxide 三氧化物、triple bond 三键、trivalent 三价的、iodine trichloride 三氯化碘、triangle 三角形

ter-三：ter-valent/trivalent 三价的、tertiary 第三的、termonomer 三元共聚单体

可以看出 tr(i)-、ter-和 three 的同源性。

5. 四相关词汇

butyl 丁基/丁酰基、butylene 丁烯、butyl acetate 乙酸丁酯、butyrycholine 丁酰胆碱

butyr-丁：butyric acid 丁酸

qua-四：quarter 四分之一/一刻钟、quadruple 四倍的、quadrangle 四边形、quaternary 四进制的、square 广场/四边形

tetra-四：tetra/tetrahedron 四面体、tetracycline 四环素、tetrahydrofuran 四氢呋喃、carbon tetrachloride 四氯化碳

6. 五相关词汇

amyl 戊基、amyl acetate 乙酸戊酯、amyl thiocyanate 硫氰酸戊酯

penta-五：pentane 戊烷、pentanol 戊醇、pentamer 五聚物、pentagon 五边形、pentacle 五角星

pentyl 戊基、pentylene 戊烯、pentylamine 戊胺

quin-五：quintenyl 戊基、quinquephenyl 五联苯、quinquidentate 五配位基

7. 六相关词汇

hex-六：hex 六连棋/十六进制、hexose 己糖、hexyne 己炔

hexa-六：hexane 己烷、hexagon 六边形、hexamer 六聚物、hexavalent 六价的、hexamethonium 六甲铵

hexyl 己基、hexylamine 己胺、hexyl acetate 乙酸己酯

可见 hex-与 six 同源。

8. 七相关词汇

hept-七：hepta 七、heptamer 七聚物、heptagon 七边形、heptachlor epoxide 七氯环氧化物

heptyl-庚基：heptyl heptylate 庚酸庚酯、heptyl alcohol 庚醇

sept-七：septet 七重奏、september 九月（原罗马历七月）

hept-、sept-和 seven 同源，均表示七。

比较 hex-和 six，hept-和 sept，似乎 h 和 s 之间存在着某种变换，另外一个例子是 semi-和 hemi-均表示"半"。

hyper-与 super-均表示"高、超、上"之意，其中 hyper-来自古印欧词根 super-。surface 估计也与此同缘，"表面"的意思。

9. 八相关词汇

oct-八:oct 八进制、octet 八重字节、octopus 八爪鱼、octuplicate 一式八份、October十月(原罗马历八月)

octa-八:octal 八进制的、octane 辛烷、octanol 辛醇、octagon 八角形

octyl-辛基:octylamine 辛胺、octyl alcohol 辛醇

10. 九相关词汇

non-九:nonyl 壬基、nonylphenol 壬基苯酚、nonatomic 九元的

nov-:November 十一月(原罗马历九月)、novena 连续九次的祷告

nine 九、nineteen 十九、ninety 九十

11. 十相关词汇

dec-十:decade 十年、December 十二月(原罗马历十月)

decyl-十:decyl 癸基、decyl alcohol 癸醇、decyl oleate 油酸癸酯

12. 十一至二十

undecane 十一烷,其中 un-表示"一",dec-表示"十"
dodecane 十二烷/月桂烷,其中 do-表示"二",dec-表示"十"
tridecane 十三烷,其中 tri-表示"三",dec-表示"十"
tetradecane 十四烷,其中 tetra-表示"四",dec-表示"十"
pentadecane 十五烷,其中 penta-表示"五",dec-表示"十"
hexadecane 十六烷,其中 hexa-表示"六",dec-表示"十"
heptadecane 十七烷,其中 hepta-表示"七",dec-表示"十"
octadecane 十八烷,其中 octa-表示"八",dec-表示"十"
nonadecane 十九烷,其中 nona-表示"九",dec-表示"十"
从二十烷开始,数字词根开始有些不规则,但仔细比较仍可发现规律。
eicosane 二十烷,其中 eicosa-表示"二十",-cosa-表示"二十"
heneicosane 二十一烷,其中 heneicosa-表示"二十一",-cosa-表示"二十"
docosane 二十二烷,其中 do-表示"二",-cosa-表示"二十"
tricosane 二十三烷,其中 tri-表示"三",-cosa-表示"二十"
tetracosane 二十四烷,其中 tetra-表示"四",-cosa-表示"二十"

pentacosane 二十五烷,其中 penta-表示"五",-cosa-表示"二十"
hexacosane 二十六烷,其中 hexa-表示"六",-cosa-表示"二十"
heptacosane 二十七烷,其中 hepta-表示"七",-cosa-表示"二十"
octacosane 二十八烷,其中 octa-表示"八",-cosa-表示"二十"
nonacosane 二十九烷,其中 nona-表示"九",-cosa-表示"二十"

进一步比较 triacontane 三十烷、hentriacontane 三十一烷、dotriacontane 三十二烷、tritriacontane 三十三烷,可以发现它们共同的成分"-triaconta-"表示"三十"。

从三十起,基数用"aconta"为代号:triaconta 三十、tetraconta 四十、octaconta 八十、nonaconta 九十

13. 十、百、千、万及更多

十:

deca-十:decane 十烷、decade 十年、decagon 十角形

deci-十分之一:deciliter 分升、decimetre 分米

百:

hundred 百

hecto-百:hecto 百、hectoliter 百公升、hectometer 百米

cent-百:century 世纪/百年

centi-百分之一/百:cent 一分、centiliter 厘升、centimeter 厘米

在单词 centipede 蜈蚣中,centi-表示"百",-pede 表示"足"。

千:

thousand 千

kilo-千:kilo 千克、kiloliter 千升、kilogram 公斤、kilometer 公里、kilowatt 千瓦

mill-千:millenary 千年、million 百万(一千个一千)

milli-千分之一:milliter 毫升、millimeter 毫米、millisecond 毫秒

万:

myriad-万:myria 万、myriad 一万/无数、myriagram 万克

百万/兆:

million 百万、percent per million (ppm)百万分之一/10^{-6}/微

mega-百万:megawatt 兆瓦、megacity 大城市、megabyte 兆字节

micro-极小的/10^{-6}:micron/micrometer 微米、microliter 微升、microscope 显微镜、microbe 微生物

十亿或更多:

billion 十亿、parts per billions（ppb）十亿分之一/10^{-9}
nano 纳/10^{-9}/毫微/十亿分之一：nanoliter（nL）纳升、nanometer 纳米
pico 皮/微微/10^{-12}：picoliter 皮升
femto-千万亿分之一/10^{-15}：femtogram(fg)飞克
attomole 阿摩尔/10^{-18} mol

表5.2介绍了一些不同前缀的缩写及其含义。

表 5.2

前缀	缩写	含义	举例
mega-	M	10^6	1 megmeter (Mm) = 10^6 m
kilo-	k	10^3	1 kilometer (km) = 10^3 m
deci-	d	10^{-1}	1 decimeter (dm) = 10^{-1} m
centi-	c	10^{-2}	1 centimeter (cm) = 10^{-2} m
milli-	m	10^{-3}	1 milligram (mg) = 10^{-3} g
micro-	μ	10^{-6}	1 microgram (μg) = 10^{-6} g
nano-	n	10^{-9}	1 nanogram (ng) = 10^{-9} g
pico-	p	10^{-12}	1 picogram (pg) = 10^{-12} g
femto-	f	10^{-15}	1 femtogram (fg) = 10^{-15} g

angstrom 埃：缩写为 A，意为 10^{-10} 米。

14. 伯仲叔季

胺是氨的氢原子被烃基代替后的有机化合物。氨分子中的一个、两个或三个氢原子被烃基取代而生成的化合物，分别称为第一胺（伯胺）、第二胺（仲胺）和第三胺（叔胺）。它们的通式为：RNH_2 伯胺、R_2NH 仲胺、R_3N 叔胺。铵离子中的四个氢原子都被烃基取代形成的化合物，称为季铵盐，通式 R_4N^+。

  primary amine 伯胺、primary carbon 伯碳
  secondery amine 仲胺、secondary carbon 仲碳
  tertiary amine 叔胺、tertiary carbon 叔碳
  quaternary amine 季胺、quatemary ammonium salt 季铵盐、quaternary carbon 季碳、quaternary alloy 四元合金

15. 星期

Monday 星期一,月曜日,故与 moon 有关

Tuesday 星期二,火曜日,对应火星和北欧战神 Tyr

Wednesday 星期三,水曜日,对应水星和日耳曼主神 Woden,译自罗马神话中的 Mercury 墨丘利

Thursday 星期四,木曜日,对应木星和北欧雷神 Thor

Friday 星期五,金曜日,对应金星和北欧爱与美女神 Frigg

Saturday 星期六,土曜日,对应土星和罗马神话农神 Saturn

Sunday 星期天,日曜日,对应太阳神和日耳曼神话 solis

16. 月份

在表示月份的词汇中可以发现一个奇怪的现象,九月 September 的词根 sept-表示"七",十月 October 的词根 octo-表示"八",十一月 November 的词根 nov-表示"九",十二月 December 的词根 dec-表示"十"。

公历一年有十二个月,起源于古罗马历法。罗马原来只有十个月,古罗马皇帝决定增加两个月放在年尾,后来朱里斯·凯撒大帝把这两个月移到年初,成为一月、二月,原来的一月、二月便成了三月、四月,依次类推。这就是今天世界沿用的公历。因此 September、October、November 和 December 分别是原来的七月、八月、九月和十月。

6 程度词汇

1. 大小

macro-大：macromolecule 大分子、macrocosm 宏观世界、macrophages 巨噬细胞

micro-小/微：micro 小、microliter 微升、microbe 微生物、microscope 显微镜、microchip 微芯片、microcomputer 微型计算机、micrometer 微米、microorganism 微生物、microwave 微波

mini-微小的：minim 滴/滴量、miniature 微型的、minimum 最小量、minor 较小的/不重要的、minus 减去、miss 未达到

> 字母 M 构成的词汇很多与数量、数字有关。
> 表示多的词有：
> many 许多的、much 较多的、massive 大量的、more 更多的、most 最多的、major 较多的、manifold 多样的、maximum 最大量、measure 测量、metric 公制的、metropolitan 大城市的、macro-大的、macromolecule 大分子、millionaire 百万富翁、milometer 计程器、main 主要的、majesty 雄伟、multi-多、multilingual 多语言的、multiply 乘/增殖、multitude 许多、amass 积聚、mega-百万的词根、megacity 人口过百万的城市、megaphone 扩音器、megalomania 自大狂、magnify 放大的、magnate 富豪/巨头、magnanimous 宽宏大量的
>
> 梵语和英语同属印欧语系，关系极为密切，佛教中的摩诃（mah-/maha）一词与英语词根 macro-应属同源。摩诃般若意为大智慧，摩诃迦叶意为伟大的迦叶尊者、摩诃衍那意为大乘佛教。
>
> mass 大块的、amass 积累、massacre 大屠杀
> mount 登上/上升/增加、mountain 山、amount 总数
> ample 数量多的/面积大的、amplify 放大、amplitude 广大/广阔
> 表示中间状态的有：
> meso-中间的、mesoporous 介孔的、mezzo 中/半、mid-……中的、middle 中间的、middling 二流的、midnight 午夜、midsummer 仲夏、midwife 接生婆、mild 温和的、moderate 适度的、moderator 调解人、moiety 一半

> 表示小、少的有：
>
> minim 滴/滴量、micro-微，来自希腊字母μ、microbe 微生物、microchip 微芯片、microcomputer 微型计算机、micrometer 微米、microorganism 微生物、microscopy 显微镜、microwave 微波、mini-微小的、miniature 微型的、minimum 最小量、minor 较小的/不重要的、minus 减去、miss 未达到、milligram 毫克、millimeter 毫米
>
> mono-单的、monochrome 单色的、monocular 单筒的、monody 独唱颂歌、monogamy 一夫一妻的、monolith 独块巨石的、monologue 独白、monomania 单一狂/偏执狂、monophonic 单声道的、monopolize 垄断、monotheism 一神教、monorail 单轨铁路、monoxide 一氧化物
>
> math 数学、mathematician 数学家、measure 测量

2. 高低

hyper-高/超：hyperoxide 超氧化物、hyperglycemia 高血糖、hypertension 高血压、hype 过度宣传、hyperacid 酸度过高的

hypo-低/次：hypoglycemia 低血糖、hypothermia 低体温、hypodermic 皮下的

hypochlorous acid 次氯酸、sodium hypochlorite 次氯酸钠、sodium hyposulfite/hypo 硫代硫酸钠

3. 多、过、超、高

multi-多：multiply 乘/繁殖、multitude 大量的、multichain 多链的、multinucleate 多核的、multicistronic mRNA 多顺反子、mRNA multicopy 多拷贝

ple/-ple/-ble 倍：double 双倍、multiple 多倍的、complex 复杂的、plenty 满的、complete 完全的、aplenty 大量、ample 广大的、amplify 放大、triple 三倍的、duple 二倍的、duplicate 复制

由"倍"衍生出"全、多"的意思：plenary 全体出席的、plenitude 充分、plentiful 丰富的、plenum 全体会议

pero-过：peroxide 过氧化物、peroxidase 过氧化物酶

per-高：perchloric acid 高氯酸、chloric acid 氯酸

poly-多：polymer 聚合物、polyester 聚酯、polygon 多边形、polytechnic 综合技艺的

super-/supra-超/多：superior 较高的、supramolecular 超分子

ultra-超：ultrasonic 超生的、ultraviolet 紫外、ultrafiltration 超滤

4. 低

infra-低：infrared 红外的

oligo-少：oligonucleotide 寡核苷酸、oligomer 低聚物、oligomerization 低聚反应

sub-下/低/小：suborder 亚目、submucosa 黏膜下层、subclone 亚克隆、subcellular 亚细胞、subsection 小节/分部

5. 半/中

centri-半：center 中心、centrifuge 离心、centriole 中心粒、centrosome 中心体、centrogeng 着丝基因

demi-半：demigod 半人半神、demibariel 半桶

hemi-半：hemisphere 半球、hemiplegia 半身麻痹

semi-半：semimonthly 半月刊、semiconductor 半导体、semicircle 半圆

meso-中间的：mesoporous 介孔的、mesosphere 中间层

med-/mid-中间：mediate 介导、middle 中部、middling 二流的、midnight 午夜、midsummer 仲夏、midwife 接生婆、mild 温和的

mo-中：moderate 适度的、moderator 调解人、moiety 一半

6. 全

holo 全/整体/完全：holoenzyme 全酶、holoprotein 全蛋白、holocrine 全质分泌、whole 全部的/全体的

pan-完全：Pan-American Airlines 泛美航空、panorama 全景、panacea 万能药、panavision 宽荧幕电影、panagglutination 全凝集、pancytopenia 全血细胞减少

al-全：all 全部、altogether 全部地/完全地、always 总是、allocate 分配、almost 几乎、almighty 全能的、all-encompassing 无所不包的、all-konwing 全知的

omni-全：omniscient 全知的、omnipresent 无所不在的

7 位置词汇

1. 邻间对

o-/ortho-邻/正位：o-phenylenediamine 邻苯二胺、orthodox 正统的/原硅酸 orthosilicic acid

m-/meta-间位：m-phenylenediamine 间苯二胺、metasilicic acid 偏硅酸

p/para- 对位：p-phenylenediamine 对苯二胺

> para-为对位、对岸、穿越、超越之意，故有 parallel 平行的、paramount 至高的，佛教语言菠萝蜜 paramita 即为超越数量、无量、到彼岸之意。

2. 左右

levo- 左：levo 左旋的、levothyroxine 左甲状腺素

levo-词根应与 left 相关。

dextro- /dexter- 右：dexter 右侧的、dextrose 葡萄糖

chirality 手性、chiro 手、chiral 手性的、achira 非手性的

3. 内外

inter-不同事物之间：intermolecular 分子间的、inter-school 校与校之间

intra-同一事物内部各部分之间：intramolecular 分子内的、intra-school 校内各队之间

intro-/endo-向内的：introversion 内向性、endothermic 吸热的

extra-/extro-/exo-向外的：extracurricular 课外的、exothermic 放热的

vivo 体内

vitro 体外/试管内

> 字母 v 和 f 常常互转，很多与生命有关：
> life 生命、live 生活、living 活着的/永生的
> female 雌性的、fertile 肥沃的/能繁殖的、fertilize 使受精、fanny 女性生殖器、fetal 胎儿、infant 婴儿

verve 生命力、vigor 活力/精力、vital 生命的/生死攸关的、vivid 生动的、in vivo在体内的

verve 生命力、vigor 活力/精力、vital 生命的/生死攸关的、vivid 生动的、in vivo在体内的 vitamin 维生素,vita-表示生命,-amin 表示氨基酸,因为最早认为维生素含有氨基酸。

字母 f 开头或者含有 f 的许多单词具有浮、轻、像水、火、光一样流出或发射等相关的含义：

fire 发/火、flicker 闪烁、flighty 轻浮的/反复的、float 浮、fly 飞、flight 飞行、flame 火焰、flare 燃烧/发怒、flash 闪耀、flood 洪水、flow 流动、flowing 流利的、fluent 流利的、fluid 液体、flutter 飘动、fluvial 河流的、fluctuate 波动、foam 泡沫、fog 雾、ford 河流浅水处、fountain 喷泉、froth 泡沫、fume 烟/气、fuse 融化、effuse 流出、effluent 流出的/发射的、infuse 灌输/浸渍

字母 f 和羽毛、叶片或者其他类似片状的物体有关：

feather 羽毛、fur 皮毛、fuzz 绒毛、fetlock 丛毛、fledged 羽毛长成的、fleece 羊毛、fluff 软毛/无价值的东西、fluffy 有绒毛的/空洞的、fringe 毛边、frizzle 卷毛、flutter 拍翅、flush 惊飞

flora 植物群、floral 花的、floret 小花、flower 花、foliate 有叶的、foliage 叶子、folio 一张、foil 叶片/金片、frond 蕨类或棕榈叶子、fruit 水果、forest 森林

flake 小薄片、film 薄膜

fern 蕨类、fescue 羊茅、fir 冷杉

farm 农场、field 土地、fertile 肥沃的

flag 旗子、flexible 弯曲的、flourish 茂盛地生长

4. 原异

in situ/in site 原位

ex situ 移位/非原位

5. 顺反

cis-顺式：cis-2-butene 顺式-2-丁烯

trans-反式：trans-2-butene 反式-2-丁烯

trans-词根对应汉语"穿、传、转"之意，如 transfer 转让、transport 传送、transform 变换、transparent 透明的。

T 开头的单词很多有交叉、穿越、交通、转换等含义：

triffic 交通、travel 旅行、traverse 横贯、treason 叛逆、trans-横跨/穿越/交互、transit 运输、transmit 传递、transfuse 输血、transparent 透明、transaction 交易、transducer 换能器、transfer 转移、transport 运输

8 词汇分析

1. 从"糖"说起

比较单词 glucose 葡萄糖、glycine 甘氨酸、glycerol 甘油,我们不妨大胆地想一想,这几个单词开头都是 gl-,那么它们之间有相关性吗？仔细比较,它们的共同之处就呼之欲出了。

glue 胶黏物,是黏性的;glutamic acid/glutamate 谷氨酸与 glue 有相同词源,因为谷氨酸从面粉中提取,而面粉也是黏性的;glutin 明胶,是黏性的;glucose 葡萄糖,糖通常是黏性的。

glycine 甘氨酸,有甜味,所以翻译为"甘";glycol 甘油,有甜味,在食品中常用作甜味剂;glycogen 糖原、glycolysis 糖酵解、hyperglycemia 高血糖。

由此可见,glu-或者 gly-均有黏性、糖、甜味相关的含义。

再仔细分析 glucose,其实不仅仅 glu-表示糖,下面的-ose 也表示糖:

glucose 葡萄糖、fructose 果糖、sucrose 蔗糖、galactose 半乳糖

还有一些物质中文名字中没有糖字,但实际上是多糖,如:

amolyse 直连淀粉、cellulose 纤维素

saccharide 糖类、monosaccharide/monose 单糖、polysaccharose/polyose 多糖

chitosan 壳聚糖

glutaraldehyde 戊二醛,一种对氨基具有交联特性的分子,其中 glutara-表示黏性的意思,-aldehyde,醛,原意为醇的脱氢产物,-de-为脱去,-hyde 是氢。

相似地,gel 凝胶,也有胶黏之意;sol gel 溶胶凝胶;gelatin 凝胶/明胶。

2. 一"石"激起千层浪

-ite 岩石/矿:ammonite 菊石、bauxite 铝土矿、calcite 方解石、cuprite 赤铜矿、granite 花岗岩、graphite 石墨、magnetite 磁铁矿

granite 花岗岩,其中 gran-来自拉丁语 granum,表示 grain"谷物",衍生出"小颗粒"的意思,因为花岗岩常能形成发育良好、肉眼可辨的矿物颗粒,由此得名。

有趣的是,很多炸药的单词也用-ite 词尾,也许是因为用于炸岩石:

ballistite 无烟火药、carbonite 碳质炸药/硝酸甘油、cheddite 谢德炸药、cyclonite 旋风炸药、dunnite 苦味酸铵火药、dynamite 炸药/破坏、tonite 棉火药、lyddite 立德炸药

另外一个和石头有关的词根是-lite,来自希腊语 lithos,石头的意思,如：
coprolite 粪化石、phonolite 响岩
lithic 石头的/结石的、lithiasis 结石病
lithium 锂,因为锂最初是在矿石中发现的,而之前发现的两种碱金属都来自植物。
lithology 岩石学、lithosphere 岩石圈、lithography 石印/平版印刷/光刻法
elite 精英/掌权人物,来自拉丁语 eligere,有 election"选举"之意,前缀 e-等于 ex,表示"外、出"等义。推测该词缘自远古时代用小石子进行投票计数选择领导人。类似词汇有：
election 选举、selection 选择/评选

古人用小石子计数、画画、选举,从而派生出选举、精英、聚拢、写、画、文字、话语、宣读等含义,古印欧语 leg-、古希腊语 legein、拉丁语 legere、lectus 均有此类含义,派生词汇有：
lecture 演讲/教训、letter 字母/文字/信
lex 词/词汇、lexicon 词典/专门词汇、lexicography 词典编撰
literature 文献/文学/著作、literally 逐字地
logos 话语/思想/理念/道/逻各斯、logic 逻辑/道理/话语、logogriph 字谜、logogram 简写、monologue 独白、dialogue 对话
-ology 学：biology 生物学、graphology 笔迹学

由字母 l 和字母 r 的转换产生了 reg-词根,有刻画等原始含义产生记录、法规、正确、权威等含义,如：register 记录/登记、regal 君王的、right 正确的、regulation 规章。

3. 化学典型词根

-ant 剂：surfactant 表面活性剂、aerosol propellant 气溶胶喷雾剂、bacteriolysant 溶菌剂、decolorant 脱色剂、depressant 抑制剂、refrigerant 冷冻剂、toxicant 毒药

-ent 剂：detergent 去垢剂/去污剂、solvent 溶剂、substituent 取代基、agent 药剂、reagent 试剂

anti-抗/防止/抑制：antibacterials 抗菌剂、antibiotics 抗生素、antifungal agents 抗真菌剂

-cide 杀：aborticide 堕胎药、bactericide、fungicide 杀真菌剂、germicide 杀菌剂、insecticide/pesticide 杀昆虫剂、weedicide 除草剂

de-解/除/脱/去：deaminase 脱氨酶、decalcification 脱钙、decolorize 脱色、decomposition 分解、dehydration 脱水作用、deoxyribonucleic acid (DNA) 脱氧核糖核酸

-gen 原/剂/素/致……物质：antigen 抗原、carcinogen 致癌物、collagen 胶原、hydrogen 氢、nitrogen 氮、oxygen 氧

gene-/genito-/geno-基因/遗传：gene 基因、genesis 发生/生殖、genetic 遗传的、genocide 种族灭绝、genoconstitution 遗传体质、genotype 基因型/遗传型

lipo-脂/脂肪：lipase 脂酶、lipid(e) 脂/类脂、lipochrome 脂色素、lipophilic 亲脂性的、liposome 脂质体

-lysis 松解/溶解/水解：autolysis 自体分解/自溶、bacteriolysis 溶菌、hydrogenolysis 氢解作用、hydrolysis 水解、photolysis 光分解、pyrolysis 热解/高温分解

stereo-固/立体/实体：stereochemistry 立体化学、steroid 类固醇、sterol 固醇

syn-/sym-共同：symmetry 对称、synchronia 同时性/同步性、synthesis 合成

9　阿拉伯语中的化学词汇

有史以来,阿拉伯人一直在欧洲、非洲和亚洲之间往来贸易,他们既是文明的传递者,也是文明的集大成者。特别是阿拉伯人对香料和炼金术的追求,使得他们掌握了大量的与化学相关知识与工艺。

alchemy 炼金术,派生出 chemistry 化学。

alcohol 酒精,来自阿拉伯语,原意是一种用作眼影的粉末。那么这种粉末和酒精有什么关系呢?原来这种眼影粉末的成分是 antimony sulfide Sb_2S_3,通过升华 stibnite 辉锑矿而制得的。根据炼金术理论,这种升华所获得的产物是物质的灵魂。相似地,酒精是通过蒸馏从酒中获得的,因此也是酒的灵魂。

alembic 蒸馏器,来自阿拉伯语,甚至更古老的闪米特语。

alkali 碱,来自阿拉伯语,其中-kali 是"草木灰"的意思,因为最初的碱来自草木灰。

以上单词均以 al-开头,来自阿拉伯语的定冠词 al(the)。

soda 苏打/汽水/碳酸钠、sodium 钠,来自阿拉伯语。Soda 原意是"碳酸钠"或"碳酸氢钠",也就是俗称的"苏打"或"小苏打",因为汽水中加入碳酸氢钠以产生二氧化碳,所以也用来表示汽水。

其他来自阿拉伯语的词汇还有:

algebra 代数

aniline 苯胺、antimony 锑、average 平均、bismuth 铋、camphor 樟脑、carat 克拉、iodine 碘、jar 罐、marcasite 白铁矿、nitre 硝石、soda 苏打、sugar 糖、syrup 糖浆、coffee 咖啡、zero 零

caliper 卡钳是一种测量 caliber 口径的装置,派生出 calibration 校准、标准化、刻度、测量口径等含义,化学上常用 calibration curve 表示"标准曲线"。

字母 C 开头的很多单词具有切割、刻画的含义,对应汉语"戈、割、刻、隔、格、个、各、颗、块"等字,如:

cut 割、carve 雕刻、chop 砍/剁、chip 碎片、chisel 凿子、crash 坠毁/摔坏/破裂、crevice 缺口/裂缝、cancel 取消、cede 割让、chunk 块/厚片、sect 小块、cube 立方体、cutter 切割器、cell 细胞/小室、closet 小房间/壁橱、cubin 小屋、category 种类、carinet 顾问团、class 班级/层次/分类、clan 宗族/党派

10　炼金术七金属

在古巴比伦人的宇宙观中，围绕地球的七大行星分别是：太阳、月亮、水星、金星、火星、木星、土星；此后，希腊和罗马神话中的神祇也与此形成了一一对应的关系；炼金术士又将七大金属与之作出了对应，如表 10.1 所示。

表 10.1

中文名	缩写	英文名	拉丁名	符号	星辰	罗马神话
金	Au	gold	aurum	☉	太阳 Sun	太阳神阿波罗 Apollo
银	Ag	silver	argentum	☽	月亮 Moon	月神卢娜 Luna
汞	Hg	mercury	hydrargyrum	☿	水星 Mercury	信使墨丘利 Mercury
铜	Cu	copper	cuprum	♀	金星 Venus	爱神维纳斯 Venus
铁	Fe	iron	ferrum	♂	火星 Mars	战神玛尔斯 Mars
锡	Sn	tin	stannum	♃	木星 Jupiter	主神朱庇特 Jupiter
铅	Pb	lead	plumbum	♄	土星 Saturn	农神萨杜恩 Saturn

这七大行星构成了连接地球与天堂的七重阶梯，象征了炼金的七个步骤。对炼金术士来说，所有的金属都共有同一种物质，之所以分成那么多种类是因为其纯净度不同。这七种金属是可以互相从一种转变到另一种的，从最底层的铅转变到最高层的完美黄金。七行星、七金属、七过程的对应如表 10.2 所示。

表 10.2

行星	金属	步骤
太阳	金	coagulation 凝结
月亮	银	distillation 蒸馏
水星	汞	fermentation 发酵
金星	铜	conjunction 结合
木星	锡	seperation 分离

续表

行星	金属	步骤
火星	铁	dissolution 溶解
土星	铅	calcination 煅烧

1. 铅

铅象征炼金术的第一步——黑化阶段，也是把贱金属杀死，为了最终炼出黄金。农神 Saturn 萨杜恩是丰收之神（图 10.1），手持镰刀♄在炼金术中，象征着杀死贱金属。

土星作为一个肉眼能够看到的距离太阳最远的行星，相比其他行星，运动非常缓慢。铅具有比重大的性质，对应着土星的迟缓运动。

图 10.1

2. 锡

图 10.2

锡箔晃动时会发出类似打雷的声音，因此对应着雷神 Jupiter 朱庇特（图 10.2），其符号♃也象征着闪电。

3. 铁

iron 铁来自古印欧语，原意为"强的、有力的、神圣的"，因为铁比铜更为坚硬，作为武器更具有杀伤力，古人认为铁是上天赐予的，是神圣的。因此铁对应着罗马神话中的 Mars 战神（图 10.3）。其符号♂为战神手持的短剑和盾牌。

4. 铜

cuprum 铜因产于塞浦路斯 cyprus 得名。

金星是太阳系中除太阳和月亮外最亮的星，对应罗马神话中爱与美的女神 Venus 维纳斯，用维纳斯的铜镜♀作为符号（图 10.4）。

图 10.3

金星之神维纳斯象征爱欲、丰饶、生殖和生命，而绿色是草木的颜色，就象征生生不息的生命繁衍。铜之所以被跟金星联系起来，可能也是缘于铜盐的绿色。铜生长的绿色铜锈,俗称铜绿;提炼铜的一种重要矿石就是绿色的孔雀石;燃烧铜所发出的火焰,也呈蓝绿色。

5. 水银

hydrargyrum 水银,来自古希腊词汇 hydrargyros,其中 hydr-表示"水",argyrum 表示"银",因为水银是液态的。

图 10.4

mercury 水银来自罗马神话中神的信使墨丘利(图 10.5),因为墨丘利善于奔

图 10.5

跑,所以象征着水银流动快、易挥发和难以捉摸。符号☿是墨丘利手持的双蛇杖的样子。

墨丘利也是商人的守护神,因为古代的商人也是长途旅行者:

market 市场/交易、merchant 商人/商业

水星是太阳系八大行星中离太阳最近的一颗,也是公转最快的一个行星,因此也用擅跑的 mercury 墨丘利来命名水星。

6. 银

argentum 银,来自古印欧语词根 arg-,表示"闪白光的、银"。因为月亮☽呈现银白色,所以对应着月神(图 10.6)。

Argentina 阿根廷,意为银。

argue 争论,就是把事情给说个"明白"。

7. 金

元素 aurum 金来自古印欧语词根 aus-,表示"金、光芒"。炼金术士认为黄金和太阳同样永恒不灭、纯粹无滓、完美无缺,因此用太阳的符号☉表示金。太阳发出金色的光

图 10.6

芒,所以金元素 Au 对应着太阳神阿波罗(图 10.7)。由太阳又衍生出"权威、命令、作者、经典"等含义:

authority 权威/权利、author 作者

gold 金也来自古印欧语,表示"闪光、闪光物、金"等含义。

Aurora 曙光/黎明/曙光女神,欧若拉是罗马神话中的黎明女神,每天早晨飞向天空,向大地宣布黎明的来临。

图 10.7

11 元素命名

在欧洲,随着越来越多化学元素的发现和各国科学文化交流的日益扩大,化学家们意识到有必要统一化学元素的命名。19世纪初,瑞典化学家贝齐里乌斯首先提出,用欧洲各国通用的拉丁文来统一命名元素,从此改变了元素命名上的混乱状况。元素名称单词末尾常以-um 或者-ium 作为词根。

Na、K 等元素符号均取自拉丁文,读音时用英文名,如表 11.1 所示。

表 11.1

中文	元素符号	拉丁文名称	英文名称
钠	Na	natrium	sodium
钾	K	kalium	potassium
汞	Hg	hydrargyrum	mercury
铁	Fe	ferrum	iron
铜	Cu	cuprum	copper
铅	Pb	plumbum	lead
银	Ag	argentum	silver
金	Au	aurum	gold

1. 以地名命名

Americium 镅:美洲 America
Californium 锎:加利福尼亚州 California
Darmstadtium 鐽:德国城市 Darmstadt
Europium 铕:欧洲 Europe
Francium 钫:法国 France
Gallium 镓:法国拉丁古名 Gallia
Germanium 锗:德国 German
Hassium 镖:德国地名 Hesse

Lutetium 镥：巴黎拉丁古名 Lutetia
Strontium 锶：苏格兰村庄 Strontian
Yttrium 钇、Ytterbium 镱、Terbium 铽、Erbium 铒：瑞典小镇 Ytterby

2. 以人名命名

Copernicium 鎶：哥白尼 Nicolaus Copernicus
Curium 锔：居里夫人 Marie Skłodowska-Curie
Einsteinium 锿：爱因斯坦 Albert Einstein
Mendelevium 钔：门捷列夫 Dmitri Ivanovich Mendeleev
Nobelium 锘：诺贝尔 Alfred Bernhard Nobel
Roentgenium 铊：伦琴 Wilhelm Conrad Röntgen

3. 以神名命名

Helium 氦：古希腊神话中的太阳神，赫利俄斯 Helios
Promethium 钷：古希腊神话中偷火被处罚的神，普罗米修斯 Prometheus
硒 selenium：月亮女神 Selene

> selenite 透明石膏/月亮石、selenology 月球学、selenodesy 月面测量、selenodont 半月齿

Tantalum 钽：希腊神话中宙斯之子，坦塔洛斯 Tantalus
Thorium 钍：北欧神话中的雷神索尔 Thor
Titanium 钛：希腊神话中的巨人泰坦/提坦，Titan
冰海沉船 Titanic 泰坦尼克号也是以此命名，以象征其巨大的身形

4. 以星宿命名

Cerium 铈：谷神星
Neptunium 镎：海王星
Palladium 钯：智神星
Plutonium 钚：冥王星
Uranium 铀：天王星

5. 以元素特性命名

Argon 氩：原义懒惰、不活泼

Sulfur 硫：原义鲜黄

Beryllium 铍：变白

Bismuth 铋：原义白色物质

Chromium 铬：原义颜色、彩色，与 colour 同源，衍生词汇如 chromatography 色谱。

> chromophore 生色基团、chromosome 染色体、chromatography 色谱法、cytochrome 细胞色素、nonochromatic 单色/单色光的

6. 以数字命名

如第 147 号元素 Unquadseptium，其中 un-表示"一"、-quad-表示"四"、-sept-表示"七"，词尾-ium 代表"元素"的意思。

12 常用元素词根

下面介绍一些常用元素词根及其衍生词汇。

1. hydrogen/H 氢

hydro-希腊词根,表示"水"的意思,-gen 表示"产生、来自"。hydrogen 氢意为"来自水的"。

hydrocarbon 碳氢化合物/烃、hydrochloric acid 氢氯酸/盐酸、hydrogen peroxide 过氧化氢、hydrolysis 水解、hydroxide 氢氧化物、hydrophobic 疏水的、hydrothermal 水热的、hydroxyl 氢氧基/羟基

2. carbon/C 碳

carbon monoxide 一氧化碳、carbohydrate 碳水化合物(比较 hydrocarbon 碳氢化合物)、carbonate 碳酸盐、polycarbonate 聚碳酸酯
carbonyl 羰基、carboxylate 羧酸盐

3. nitrogen/N 氮

nitric acid 硝酸、nitrate 硝酸盐
nitrous acid 亚硝酸、nitrous oxide 一氧化二氮/氧化亚氮
nitroglycerin 硝酸甘油

4. oxygen/O 氧

oxidation/ oxidization 氧化、oxidize 使氧化、oxidative stress 氧化应激
oxide 氧化物、oxidant 氧化剂、antioxidant 抗氧化剂、oxidase 氧化酶
carbon dioxide 二氧化碳、hydroxide 氢氧化物
redox 氧化还原,由 reduction 还原+oxidation 氧化两个词组成。
anoxic 无氧的,其中前缀 an-表示"无"。

5. natrium/sodium/Na 钠

sodium 钠来自 soda 苏打,因为钠元素最初分离自苛性苏打(氢氧化钠)。
natrium 钠来自苏打的一种,natron 泡碱。
natrolite 钠沸石、natroalunite 钠明矾石
sodium chloride 氯化钠、sodium hydroxide 氢氧化钠

6. magnesium/Mg 镁和 manganese/Mn 锰

magnesium/Mg 镁和 Mn/manganese 锰,都来自古希腊词源 magnesia 氧化镁,哲人石或者叫做魔法石的主要成分,与 magnet 磁铁、magnetite 磁铁矿也有关。

从 magnetic 磁性的和 magic 魔力的/有吸引力的这两个词的相关性可以看出古人认为磁性具有魔力般的作用。

7. silicon/Si 硅

silica 二氧化硅、silica gel 硅胶
silicon valley 硅谷、silicon carbide 碳化硅、silicon chip 硅片、silicon dioxide 二氧化硅
silicone 硅酮、silicon rubber 硅橡胶
silicate 硅酸盐

8. sulfur/S 硫

sulfate 硫酸盐、sulfite 亚硫酸盐
sulfation 硫化作用、sulfonate 磺化
sulfide 硫化物
sulfur dioxide 二氧化硫、sulfuric acid 硫酸、sulfurous 硫黄的
sulphur 硫黄
有三个词根均与"硫"相关,surfur-、merca-、thio-:
硫醇 sulfur alcohol/mercaptan/thiol/thioalcohol
巯基 sulfhedryl/sulfhydryl group/mercapto/thiol/hydrosulphonyl/hydrosulfuryl
mercapturic acid 硫醇尿酸,其中 mercapt-表示"硫",-uric 表示"尿"。
mercaptocarboxylic acid 巯基羧酸

thiourea 硫脲、thiophene 硫代呋喃/噻吩、thioester 硫酯、thiocyanate 硫氰酸盐

9. chlorine/Cl 氯

来自希腊词源 khloros,表示"淡绿",因此有缺少"绿色"之意,中文"氯"字的读音显然也与此相关。

chloride 氯化物、chlorophyll 叶绿素、chloroform 氯仿、chlorosis 缺氯症、chlorobenzene 氯苯

10. kalium/K/potassium 钾

potassium 钾来自拉丁词汇 potash 碳酸钾/草碱,因为戴维从草碱中分离出钾元素。

kalium 钾来自阿拉伯词汇 al-qaliy,表示"灰烬"之意。alkali 碱也来自同一个词源。

11. calcium 钙

calcium 来自拉丁词源 calx,表示 limestone 石灰岩的意思。

chalk 白垩/粉笔也来自 calx,白垩是碳酸钙的沉积物。

calcium carbonate 碳酸钙

calcination 煅烧,该词应和石灰的制造工艺有关;石灰是用石灰石、白云石、白垩、贝壳等碳酸钙含量高的产物,经高温煅烧而成。

calcification 钙化、calcific 钙化的

calcite 方解石

---

cal-, car-, cer-来自古印欧词源,与"热、烧"有关:

calorie 卡路里/大卡(热量单位)

calorimeter 量热器

carbon 碳(烧制而成的)

ceramic 陶器(烧制而成的)

---

12. ferrum/iron/Fe 铁

ferrite 铁氧体、ferritin 铁蛋白

ferro- 含铁的、ferromagnetic 铁磁的、ferrocene 二茂铁
ferrous 二价铁的、ferrous sulfate 硫酸亚铁
ferric 三价铁的、ferric chloride 三氯化铁
ferrocyanide 亚铁氰化物、ferricyanide 铁氰化物

> 另一个与铁有关的词根是 heme-或者 hemo-,原意为"血",可能与古人祭祀时用 hematite 赤铁矿象征血液有关,后来衍生出血红素铁的含义:
> hematite 赤铁矿、heme 亚铁血红素、protoheme 正铁血红素、hemoglobin 血红素/血红蛋白

13. cobalt/Co 钴

cobalt blue 钴蓝、cobalt dichloride 二氯化钴

14. nickel/Ni 镍

nickel-plated 镀镍的、nickel alloy 镍合金

15. coprum/copper/Cu 铜

cuprate 铜酸盐
cupreous-/cupro- 含铜的
cupric oxide/copper oxide 氧化铜、cupric ion 铜离子
cuprous 亚铜/一价铜的、cuprous oxide 氧化亚铜
cuprite 赤铜矿

16. zincum/zinc/Zn 锌

zinc oxide 氧化锌、zinc phosphate 磷酸锌

17. bromine/Br 溴

bromide 溴化物、bromophenol 溴苯酚、bromobutane 溴丁烷

18. ruthenium/Ru 钌

因采自俄罗斯 Russa 而得名。
ruthenium tetroxide 四氧化钌

19. rhodium/Ru 铑

rhodium black 铑黑

rhodium 铑来自希腊词汇 rhodon，意为 rose 玫瑰色，因铑盐的溶液呈现玫瑰的淡红色彩而得名。

rhodamine 罗丹明/玫瑰精也来自同样词源。

rhodolite 红榴石、rhodonite 玫瑰石

比较以上词汇，可以发现都与玫瑰红的颜色相关。

20. palladium/Pd 钯

Palladium 还有守护神之意。来自希腊神话女神 Pallas 帕拉斯的名字，她是特里同之女，利比亚特里托尼斯湖的水泽神女，雅典娜在和她玩战争游戏时因长矛的一击被宙斯用神盾挡住了而分心，被雅典娜失手杀死，雅典娜非常悔恨，因而改名为帕拉斯·雅典娜。

21. argentum/silver/Ag 银

argentum 来自古印欧语，愿意为白色、闪光。

argentometry 银滴定法、argentite 辉银矿

Argentina 阿根廷，意为银。

argue 争论，就是使"明白"，因为 arg-词根也有像银一样亮、白的意思。

silver screen 银幕、silverware 银器、silversmith 银匠

22. cadmium/Cd 镉

cadmium plating 镀镉

23. indium/In 铟

indium-tin oxide glass (ITO)氧化铟锡玻璃，即导电玻璃。

24. stannum/tin/Sn 锡

stannum 是 tin 的拉丁语。

stannous 锡的、stannate 锡酸盐、stannane 锡烷

tin 锡、镀锡、罐头、听/罐

25. stibonium/antimony/Sb 锑

stibonium salt 四氢锑盐
antimony trioxide 三氧化锑

26. tellurium/Te 碲

tellurite 亚锑酸盐/黄锑矿

27. iodine/I 碘

来自古希腊词源 ioeides，表示紫色、紫罗兰。
iodine 碘/碘酒
iodide 碘化物、iodate 用碘处理、iodine value 碘值

28. platinum/Pt 铂

platinum 来自古法语，与 plate 同源，表示金属片。
plate 金属片/金属板/盘子/电镀
plat-平/片/块：plat 小块地、platform 站台/平台、plateau 高原/台地、platelet 薄片/血小板、platter 唱片、platitude 平凡
由于 p 和 f 的音转：flat 平的/平面。

29. aurum/gold 金

aurum 是 gold 的拉丁词。
auriferous 产金的、aureate 镀金的/灿烂的
gold 金与 glass 玻璃都来自古印欧语词根 ghel-，表示发光、光滑、金等含义。相似词汇如：
glacier 冰河/冰川、glass 玻璃
glance/glimpse 闪微光/一瞥、glare 发强光/怒视
gleam 闪耀/闪光
glitter 闪耀/吸引力、glide 滑行/掠过、glitch 一闪/脉冲/小错误、glimmer 微光/模糊感觉/隐约出现、glisten 闪耀/闪光、glint 闪耀/飞出
glow 发光/白热/脸红、glory 光荣/骄傲、gloomy 黑暗的、gloss 光彩/假象/掩饰

30. hydrargyrum/mercury/Hg 汞

hydrargyrum 来自希腊语 hydrargyros,其中 hydr-表示水,argyros 表示银。
mercury 来自罗马神话中的 Mercury 墨丘利,是商业保护神、信使、炼金术和医疗保护神。
merchandise 商品/经商、merchant 商人、market 市场

31. plumbum/lead/Pb 铅

铅比较重,常用作铅垂线,用于拉垂直线或者探测。
plumb 铅垂/探测/垂直/铅管、plumber 管子工
plummet 铅锤/坠落

13 无机化学命名

化学词汇命名系统命名法(nomenclature)由国际纯粹与应用化学联合会(International Union of Pure and Applied Chemistry, IUPAC)制定。在实际应用中,传统命名方法常常和系统命名法混用。

1. 阳离子 cations

H^+	hydrogen ion	Mg^{2+}	magnesian ion	Al^{3+}	aluminum ion
Li^+	lithium ion	Ca^{2+}	calcium ion		
Na^+	sodium ion	Ba^{2+}	barium ion		
K^+	potassium ion	Zn^{2+}	zinc ion		
Ag^+	silver ion	Cd^{2+}	cadmium ion		
NH_4^+	ammonium ion				
H_3O^+	hydronium				

如 KCl 氯化钾 potassium chloride、$Mg(NO_3)_2$ 硝酸镁 magnesium nitrate。

2. 不同氧化态阳离子

Fe^{2+}	iron(Ⅱ)或 ferrous	Pb^{2+}	lead(Ⅱ)或 plumbousl
Fe^{3+}	iron(Ⅲ)或 ferric	Pb^{4+}	lead(Ⅳ)或 plumbic
Cr^{2+}	chromium(Ⅱ)或 chromous	Cu^+	copper(Ⅰ)或 cuprous
Cr^{3+}	chromium(Ⅲ)或 chromic	Cu^{2+}	copper(Ⅱ)或 cupric
Sn^{2+}	tin(Ⅱ)或 stannous	Hg^+	mercury(Ⅰ)或 mercurous
Sn^{4+}	tin(Ⅳ)或 stannic	Hg^{2+}	mercury(Ⅱ)或 mercuric

以铁离子为例:
ferro-亚铁:ferrocyanide 亚铁氰化物、ferrocene 二茂铁
ferric-三价铁:ferricyanide 铁氰化物、ferric chloride 三氯化铁

3. 阴离子和盐

后缀-ide 用来表示单原子阴离子。

H$^-$ hydride	Cl$^-$ chloride	F$^-$ chloride
Br$^-$ bromide	I$^-$ iodide	O^{2-} oxide
S^{2-} sulfide	N^{3-} nitride	C^{4-} carbide
CN$^-$ cyanide	OH$^-$ hydroxide	

如 NaCl 为 sodium chloride，CaF$_2$ 为 calcium fluoride。

NO$_3^-$ nitrate	SO$_4^-$ sulfate	CO$_3^{2-}$ carbonate	PO$_4^{3-}$ phosphate
CrO$_4^{2-}$ chromate	BO$_3^{3-}$ borate	SCN$^-$ thiocyanate	MnO$_4^-$ permanganate

如 NaNO$_3$ 硝酸钠 sodium nitrate、CaCO$_3$ 碳酸钙 calcium carbonate。

4. 二元化合物

SO$_2$	SO$_3$	SF$_4$	Cl$_2$O$_7$
sulfur dioxide	sulfur trioxide	sulfur tetrafluoride	dichlorine heptoxide

5. 酸和盐

HF hydrofluoric acid	HCl hydrochloric acid	HBr hydrobromic acid	HI hydroiodic acid
HCN hydrocyanic acid	H$_2$S hydrosulfuric acid	H$_2$CO$_3$ carbonic acid	
KH$_2$PO$_4$ potassium dihydrogen phosphate		K$_2$HPO$_4$ dipotassium hydrogen phosphate	

Ternary acid: An acid containing three elements: H, O, and (usually) another nonmetal.

三元酸：含有三个元素的酸，通常是 H，O 和另一个非金属。

对于具有不同氧化态的含氧酸及其盐可以命名如表 13.1 所示。

表 13.1

高/过	正	亚	次
酸 per- -ic 盐 per- -ate	酸 -ic 盐 -ate	酸 -ous 盐 -ite	酸 hypo- -ous 盐 hypo- -ite
$HClO_4$ 高氯酸 perchloric acid ClO_4^- 高氯酸盐 perchlorate	$HClO_3$ 氯酸 chloric acid ClO_3^- 氯酸盐 chlorate	$HClO_2$ 亚氯酸 chlorous acid ClO_2^- 亚氯酸盐 chlorite	$HClO$ 次氯酸 hypochlorous acid ClO^- 次氯酸盐 hypochlorite
	HNO_3 硝酸 nitric acid NO_3^- 硝酸盐 nitrate	HNO_2 亚硝酸 nitrous acid NO_2^- 亚硝酸盐 nitrite	
	H_2SO_4 硫酸 sulfuric acid SO_4^{2-} 硫酸盐 sulfate	H_2SO_3 亚硫酸 sulfurous acid SO_3^{2-} 亚硫酸盐 sulfite	

含氧酸根的化合价与其中氧原子数相同的酸,称为原酸,如 H_4SiO_4 原硅酸 orthosilicic acid。

偏酸正酸缩去一分子水而成的酸,称为偏某酸。例如:H_2SiO_3 偏硅酸 metasilicic acid。

焦酸(重酸)由两个简单含氧酸缩去一分子水,通常命名为焦酸,也有称重酸。如:

$2H_2SO_4 - H_2O = H_2S_2O_7$(焦硫酸 disulfuric acid/pyrosulfuric acid)

$2H_2CrO_4 - H_2O = H_2Cr_2O_7$(重铬酸 dichromic acid/bichromic acid)

> pyro-焦/火/热,古希腊词根,与 fire 同源,有"火、热"含义,在化学上常翻译为"焦",可能与加热脱水有关,如:
>
> pyrogen 热原、pyrolysis 热解、pyrophosphate 焦磷酸、pyrogallol 焦酚/邻苯三酚/焦性没食子酸
>
> pyrometer 高温计、pyroelectricity 热电、pyromania 纵火狂
>
> pyrexia 发热、antipyretic 退热的/解热剂

Acid anhydride: A nonmetal oxide that reacts with water to form an acid.

酸酐：与水反应能生成酸的非金属氧化物。

6. 碱

Basic anhydride: A metal oxide that reacts with water to form a base.

碱酐：与水反应生成碱的金属氧化物。

Amphoteric oxide: An oxide that shows some acidic and some basic properties.

两性氧化物：既有酸性、又有碱性的氧化物。

14 有机化学命名

1. 烷烃 alkane

(1) 直链烷烃

-ane 烷烃：methane 甲烷、ethane 乙烷、propane 丙烷、butane 丁烷、pentane 戊烷、hexane 己烷、heptane 庚烷、octane 辛烷、nonane 壬烷、decane 癸烷

-yl 烷基：methyl-甲基、ethyl-乙基、pentyl-丙基

(2) 支链烷烃

按照烷烃分子碳原子所连接的其他碳原子的个数不同，可分别称为：

secondary carbon 仲碳原子 2°
tertiary carbon 叔碳原子 3°
quaternary carbon 季碳原子 4°
sec-butyl 仲丁基
tert-butyl 叔丁基
n-/normal/正：n-butyl 正丁基
i-/ iso/异：isobutyl 异丁基
neo/新：neopentane 新戊烷

(3) 环烷烃 cycloalkane

cyclo...ane 环…烷：cyclopropane 环丙烷、cyclobutane 环丁烷、cyclopentane 环戊烷、cyclohexane 环己烷、methylcyclohexane 甲基环己烷

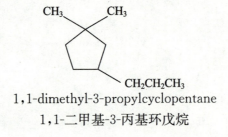

1,1-dimethyl-3-propylcyclopentane
1,1-二甲基-3-丙基环戊烷

2. 烯烃 alkene 和烯基 -enyl

-ene 烯烃:ethylene 乙烯、cyclopropene/cyclopropylene 环丙烯、butene 丁烯
-diene 二烯:butadiene 丁二烯
-triene 三烯:butatriene 丁三烯
-tetraene 四烯:cyclooctatetraene 环辛四烯

3. 异构

geometrical isomerism 几何异构、stereo-isomerism 立体异构、Z,E-isomerism Z,E 异构、cis-trans-isomerism 顺反异构、configurational isomerism 构型异构、optical isomerism 光学旋光异构

cis-顺式:cis-2-butene 顺式-2-丁烯
trans-反式:trans-2-butene 反式-2-丁烯

4. 炔烃 alkyne

-ynyl 炔基
-yne 炔烃:ethyne/acetylene 乙炔、butyne 丁炔、1-buten-3-yne 1-丁烯-3-炔
-diyne 二炔:hexadiyne/hexadiine 己二炔
-triyne 三炔

$$CH_3-CH=CH-C\equiv CH$$
3-penten-1-yne
3-戊烯-1-炔

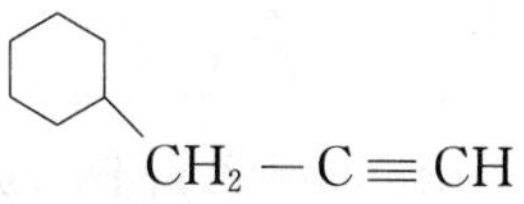

$$CH_2-C\equiv CH$$
3-cyclohexyl-1-propyne
3-环己基-1-丙炔

5. 芳香烃 aromatic hydrocarbon/arene

arom 有香味的/芳香的/芳烃的、aryl 芳基/芳基、arylate 芳基化合物
benzene 苯:phenyl 苯基、benzenyl 苯次甲基/苄川、benzyl 苯甲基/苄基、benzoyl 苯甲酰基

nitrobenzene 硝基苯、1,2,3-trimethylbenzene 1,2,3-三甲基苯、o-dichlorobenzene 邻二氯苯、p-nitrotoluene 对硝基甲苯

IUPAC 采用的俗名：toluene（methylbenzene）甲苯、phenol（benzenol）苯酚、aniline/benzenamine 苯胺、benzaldehyde/benzaldehyde 苯甲醛、benzoic acid/benzoic acid/benzene carbonic acid/benzene carboxylic acid 苯甲酸

6. 卤代烃 halogenated hydrocarbon

chloromethane/methyl chloride 氯甲烷、dichloromethane 二氯甲烷、$CHCl_3$ trichloromethane 三氯甲烷、tetrachloromethane/carbon tetrachloride 四氯化碳/四氯甲烷

7. 醇 alcohol

alcohol 一元醇：alcohol 醇/乙醇、methyl alcohol 甲醇、isopropyl alcohol 异丙醇

-anol 一元醇：methanol 甲醇、ethanol 乙醇、cyclohexanol 环己醇

-ol 多元醇：glycol 乙二醇、glycerol 甘油、1,2-ethanediol 1,2-乙二醇、cyclohexanehexaol 环六己醇

hydroxyl-羟基

8. 酚 phenol

-ol 酚：phenol/benzenol 苯酚、naphthol 萘酚、benzenediol 苯二酚、pdihydroxylbenzene 对苯二酚

9. 醇与酚盐 alkoxide

sodium ethoxide/sodium ethanolate 乙醇钠/乙氧钠、potassium phenoxide/potassium phenolate 苯酚钾

10. 醚 ether

ether 醚：diethyl ether 乙醚、ethyl methyl ether 甲乙醚、methyl n-propyl ether 甲基正丙基醚

3-methoxyphenol 3-甲氧基苯酚、1-chloro-2-chloromethoxyethane 1-氯-2-氯甲氧基乙烷、3-methoxy-2-pentanol 3-甲氧基-2-戊醇、2-methoxy-6-chloro-4-methyl-hexane 2-甲氧基-6-氯-4-甲基乙烷

crown ether 冠醚、15-crown-5 15-冠醚-5

cyclic ether 环醚按杂环化合物命名，用 oxa-、thia-、aza-、phospha-表示氧杂、硫杂、氮杂、磷杂：1,3-dithiacyclohexane 1,3-二硫环己烷、oxacyclohexane/tetralydropyran(e) 四氢吡喃

11. 醛 aldehyde

carbonyl group 羰基
传统构词从相应的酸变化而来，酸去掉-ic(-oic)acid＋-aldehyde＝某醛
formic acid 甲酸 ⇒formaldehyde 甲醛
acetic acid 乙酸 ⇒acetaldehyde 乙醛
benzoic acid 苯甲酸 ⇒benzaldehyde 苯甲醛
烃去词尾-e 加 al 表示相应的一元醛：ethanal 乙醛、3-methylbutanal 3-甲基丁醛、propenal 丙烯醛

12. 酮 ketone

-one 酮
ketone 酮、acetone/dimethyl ketone 丙酮/二甲基甲酮、ethyl methyl ketone 甲基乙基酮、methyl phenyl ketone 甲基苯丙酮
5-ethyl-3-heptanone 5-乙基-3-庚酮
3-methylcyclopentanone 3-甲基环戊酮
2,4-pentandione 2,4-戊二酮
1-acetonaphthone 萘乙酮
benzophenone/diphenyl ketone 苯甲酮

13. 醌 quinone

-quinone 醌：1,2-benzoquinone 1,2-苯醌、2,6-naphthoquinone 2,6-萘醌、9,10-anthraquinone 9,10-蒽醌、9,10-phenanthraquinone 9,10-菲醌

14. 羧酸 carboxylic acid

carboxyl 羧基
（1）简单直链羧酸

-oic acid 羧酸

HCOOH   methanoic acid/formic acid 甲酸

CH_3COOH ethanoic acid/acetic acid/acetate 乙酸

$CH_2=CHCOOH$ propenoic acid 丙烯酸

(2) 二元羧酸

-dioic acid 二羧酸

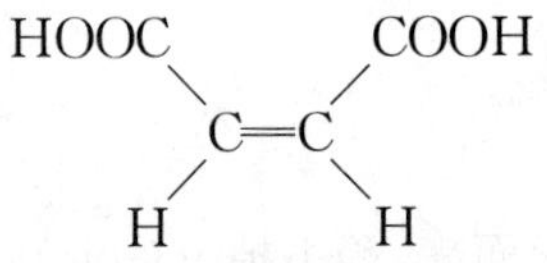

$$\underset{H}{HOOC}\diagdown C=C \diagup \underset{H}{COOH}$$

z-butenedioic acid
顺丁烯二酸

(3) 多元羧酸

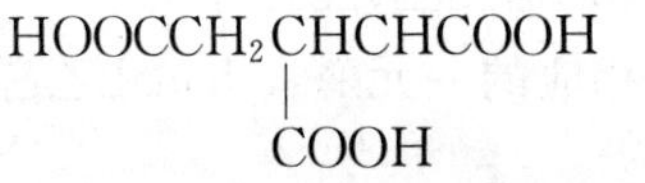

$$HOOCCH_2CHCHCOOH$$
$$|$$
$$COOH$$

propane-1,2,3-tricarboxylic acid
丙三羧酸

15. 酯 ester

醇烃基+盐词尾=酯(盐)

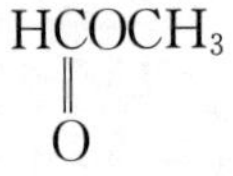

$$\underset{O}{\overset{\|}{HCOCH_3}}$$ methyl methanoate/methyl formate 甲酸甲酯

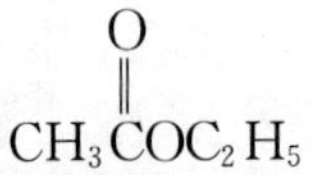

$$\underset{}{\overset{O}{\overset{\|}{CH_3COC_2H_5}}}$$ ethyl ethanoate/ethyl acetate 乙酸乙酯

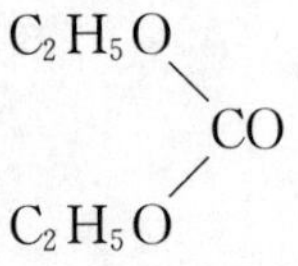

$$\underset{C_2H_5O}{\overset{C_2H_5O}{}}\!\!\diagdown CO$$ diethyl carbonate 碳酸二乙酯

$C_2H_5OSO_3H$ monoethyl sulfate/ethyl hydrogen sulfate 硫酸一乙酯

16. 酰胺 amide

-amide 酰胺、amido- 酰胺基

$$\underset{O}{\overset{\|}{HCNH_3}}$$

methanamide/formamide 甲酰胺

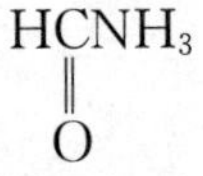

17. 胺 amine

(1) 基团
NH₃ 氨 ammonia、NH₄⁺ 铵离子 ammonium
-amine 胺、amino- 胺基:

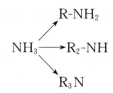

(2) 普通命名
烃基＋ -amine＝某胺
C₂H₅NH₂　　ethylamine　　乙胺
(C₂H₅)₂NH　　diethylamine　　二乙胺
C₆H₅NH₂　　phenylamine　　苯胺
(3) IUPAC 命名
　　　　　　(序号)amino-＋烃全词＝某胺

2-aminoprooane/isopropylamine　2-氨基丙烷/异丙胺　　CH₃CHCH₃
　　　　　　　　　　　　　　　　　　　　　　　　　　　　|
　　　　　　　　　　　　　　　　　　　　　　　　　　　　NH₂

18. hydrocarbyl 烃基命名

将烃类名称的词尾换为-yl, 例:
methyl 甲基、ethyl 乙基、decyl 癸基、ethenyl 乙烯基、butenyl 丁烯基、ethynyl 乙炔基、phenyl 苯基、benzyl 苄基

19. 酶

-ase 酶: urease 尿酶、glucose oxidase 葡萄糖氧化酶、peroxidase 过氧化物酶

20. "素""质""精""华"

有些经过提纯获取的物质, 特别是能形成结晶的成分, 常以-in 结尾, 翻译为"素""质""精""华"等词:
chitin 壳素/角质、insulin 胰岛素、casein 酪素
melanin 黑色素、letein 叶黄素、erythromycin 红霉素、chlorophyll 叶绿素、

aureomycin 金霉素
protein 蛋白质、chromatin 染色质
saccharin 糖精

21. 体/物

-mer 体：isomer 异构体、polymer 聚合物、dendrimer 树枝状聚合物、oligomer 低聚物/低聚体

-some：chromosome 染色体、genesome 基因体、allosome 异染色体、chondriosome 线粒体、centrosome 中心体、lipsome 脂质体

> -some 古英语词根，表示一群，常常翻译为"……体"，与 some、sum、same、similar 相关，显然，同类相聚为群，因此和下列词汇的关系不言而喻：
>
> same 同类人/同类物
>
> similar 相似的、simulate 模拟（有相似的意思）、simultaneous 同时发生的
> some 一些（有同类物质之意）
>
> sum 总数/归纳、summary 总结、resume 简历/个人总结
>
> syn-/sym- 共同：symmetry 对称、synchronia 同时性/同步性、synthesis 合成
>
> semble 看起来好像、assemble 集合/组装、self-assembled-monolayer 自组装单层
>
> 以上词义均与 sem-词根有关，也表示"半"，如 semicircle 半圆、semiconductor 半导体，可以想象，一个物体一分两半，具有彼此相似对等的含义，衍生出 semester 半学年/一学期。半年是六个月，半天是六小时，sem-可能和 six 也有一定的关联。
>
> semi-的另外一个形式是 hemi-也表示"半"，如 hemisphere 半球；hemi-和 half 也有关联。

22. 脂肪

lipid 脂质、lipid bilayer 磷脂双层、phospholipid 磷脂

liposome 脂质体、lipoprotein 脂蛋白、lipopolysaccharide 脂多糖、lipolysis 脂类分解、lipoma 脂肪瘤

15 化学基础

<u>Chemistry is the science that describes matter, its properties, the changes it undergoes, and the energy changes that accompany those processes.</u>

化学是一门科学,它研究物质及其性质、所经历的变化以及伴随这些变化所发生的能量的变化。

> science 科学的词根是 sci-来自古印欧语,表示切割、分离的含义,因为 science 是对世界的剖析,把事物分解开来仔细研究。中国早期把 science 翻译为格致,格物致知的意思,这里"格"字也是切成一小块一小块的意思,同样格致也是把事物分解开来仔细研究的意思。
>
> sci-表示切割还体现在单词 scissors 剪刀和 screen/筛子屏幕中,screen 的本义是切开分割形成的网格、格子,衍生出筛子的含义,因屏幕是由像素构成的网格,所以也用来表示屏幕的意思。
>
> 字母 s 和 c 构成的单词常有切割、刻画等含义,这两个字母也常常组合在一起衍生出如下含义:
>
> scribe 抄写员、script/manuscript 手稿、schedule 计划表、scale 刻度、scratch 刮擦、scheme 方案/计划
>
> skill 技能/本领,其本意为区别/区分/识别/判断等,字母 k 可看作字母 c 的变化
>
> Smith 作为人名常常翻译为史密斯,其原意为铁匠或以金属加工为业的手艺人,来自古印欧语词根 smi-,意为切割、用尖锐的工具加工。
>
> 由切割衍生出分离、单独等含义:solid 固体/整体、solidify 结晶/使一致、solitaire 独粒宝石、soliloquy 自言自语/独白、solipsism 唯我论、solitary 独居的、solo 独唱、soloist 单独表演者、single 单个的。

<u>Matter</u>: Anything that has mass and occupies space.

物质:是任何具有质量并占据空间的物体。

> 英国哲学家罗素曾经开玩笑说:
> What is 'matter'? Never mind!
> What is 'mind'? It doesn't matter!

Energy：The capacity to do work or transfer heat.

能量：做功或传热的能力。

An element is a chemical substance that is made up of a particular kind of atoms and hence cannot be broken down or transformed by a chemical reaction into a different element, though it can be transmutated into another element through a nuclear reaction.

元素是由一种特定原子所组成的,不能被化学反应降解为不同元素的化学纯净物,它可以通过核反应转化为另外一种物质。

> 由于"单质"和"元素"在英语中是同一个单词"element",为了加以区分,单质可以表示为：
> elementary substance/simple substance/free element：A substance composed of a single type of element.
> 单质：是由同种元素组成的纯净物。

Substance：Any kind of matter all specimens of which have the same chemical composition and physical properties.

纯净物：每一部分都有同样化学成分和物理性质的物质。

Compound：A substance composed of two or more elements in fixed proportions.

化合物：以两种或更多元素以特定比例构成的物质。

Mixture：A sample of matter composed of variable amounts of two or more substances, each of which retains its identity and properties.

混合物：是两种或几种纯净物的混合,每种纯净物保留各自的组成和性质。

Homogeneous mixture：A mixture that has uniform composition and properties throughout.

匀相混合物：具有均一组成和性质的混合物。

Heterogeneous mixture：A mixture that does not have uniform composition and properties throughout.

非匀相混合物：不具有均一组成和性质的混合物。

Law of Conservation of Matter/Law of Conservation of Mass/Principle of Mass/Matter Conservation：No detectable change occurs in the total quantity of matter during a chemical reaction or during a physical change.

质量守恒定律：在化学反应或物理变化过程中,物质的总量没有明显变化。

Law of Conservation of Energy：Energy cannot be created or destroyed in a chemical reaction or in a physical change; it may be changed from one form to another.

能量守恒定律:在化学反应或物理变化中,能量既不会凭空产生,也不会凭空消灭,它只能从一种形式转化为其他形式,或者从一个物体转移到另一个物体,总量不变。

Law of Conservation of Matter and Energy: The combined amount of matter and energy available in the universe is fixed.

质能守恒定律:宇宙中的质量和能量的总和不变。

Law of Constant Composition/Law of Definite Proportions: Different samples of any pure compound contain the same elements in the same proportions by mass.

定比定律:每一种化合物的组成元素的质量都有一定的比例关系。

Law of Multiple Proportions: When two elements, A and B, form more than one compound, the ratio of the masses of element B that combine with a given mass of element A in each of the compounds can be expressed by small whole numbers.

倍比定律:当甲、乙两种元素相互化合,能生成几种不同的化合物时,则在这些化合物中,与一定量甲元素相化合的乙元素的质量必互成简单的整数比。

Property: Characteristics that describe samples of matter.

> 在化学中有三个词常用来表述化学性质,如 property, characteristic, quality;它们之间有些微妙的区别:
> property 性质:强调事物所具有的性能、特点等,如 chemical properties 化学性质。
> characteristic 特性:强调事物与其他事物不同的特性,如 the textural characteristics of the rocks 岩石的纹理状特性;characterization 表征。
> quality 品质/质量:强调事物的优质之处,如 the quality of the products 产品的质量;与 quality 品质/质量常常混淆的 quantity 数量。

Mass: A measure of the amount of matter in an object. Mass is usually measured in grams or kilograms.

质量:指物体所含物质的多少,单位是 g 或 kg。

> Mass 表示质量和 quality 的质量含义不同,前者指多少,后者指好坏。

Weight：A measure of the gravitational attraction of the earth for a body.
重力/重量:物体由于地球的吸引而受到的力。
Temperature：A measure of the intensity of heat, that is, the hotness or coldness of a sample or object.
温度:是表示物体冷热程度的量值。
Density：Mass per unit volume.
密度:单位体积的质量。

> density/密度/稠度、densify 使密度增加
> condense 浓缩/使凝结、condensation 凝结作用

Specific gravity：The ratio of the density of a substance to the density of water at the same temperature.
比重:物质在标准条件下与水的密度比值。
Heat capacity：The amount of heat required to raise the temperature of a body (of whatever mass) one degree Celsius.
热容:把物体温度升高 1 摄氏度所需要的热量。
Specific heat：The amount of heat required to raise the temperature of one gram of a substance one degree Celsius.
比热容:在相态不变的情况下,把 1 克物质升高 1 摄氏度所需要的热量。
Calorie：Defined as exactly 4.184 joules.
卡路里:能量单位,1 卡=4.184 焦耳
Joule：A unit of energy in the SI system.
Joule 焦耳:能量单位。
Kinetic energy：Energy that matter possesses by virtue of its motion.
动能:物体由于运动而具有的能。

> kinetics 和 dynamics 都表示动力学的含义,但其中有一点微妙的差别:
> kinetic 运动的/活跃的/能动的/有力的/动力学的/运动的
> kinetics 来自古希腊词汇 kinesis,表示动或者移动,强调随着时间的变化,如:
> chemical kinetics 化学动力学,研究化学反应过程的速率和反应机理的物理化学分支学科,它的研究对象是物质性质随时间变化的非平衡的动态体系。
> enzyme kinetics 酶动力学,研究酶引起的生化反应速率。
> pharmacokinetics 药物动力学,研究药物在体内吸收、分布、代谢和排出的过程和速率。

> dynamic 动力的/动力学的/动态的
>
> dynamics 也来自古希腊词汇 dynamikos,表示有力的、力量的,强调由于受力而引起的运动或变化。如:
>
> thermodynamics 热动力学/热力学,研究热能和机械能之间的关系,研究热现象中物态转变和能量转换规律。
>
> aerodynamics 空气动力学,研究气体的运动。
>
> Brownian dynamics 布朗动力学,研究胶体粒子的布朗运动。
>
> fluid dynamics/hydrodynamics 流体动力学,研究流体的运动。
>
> molecular dynamics 分子动力学,研究分子尺度的运动。

potential energy: Energy that matter possesses by virtue of its position, condition, or composition.

势能:物体由于位置或位形而具有的能量。

> potential 还有电位、潜在的等含义。

endothermic 吸热的

> en-应和 in-相关,表示里面。
> endo-向内的:endoscopy 内镜检查术、endothelial 内皮的

exothermic 放热的

> ex-外面的:exotic 异国的/外来的/奇异的、extract 提取/拔出、exoplanet 外星球、exit 出口

Precision: How closely repeated measurements of the same quantity agree with one another.

精确性:多次等量测量的接近程度。

Accuracy: How closely a measured value agrees with the correct value.

准确性:观测值或估计值与真值的接近程度。

Significant figures: Digits that indicate the precision of measurements—digits of a measured number that have uncertainty only in the last digit.

有效数字:指在分析工作中实际能够测量到的数字,包括最后一位估计的、不确定的数字。

16 化学式与组成

Atomic mass unit (amu): One twelfth of the mass of an atom of the carbon-12 isotope.

原子质量单位:碳-12同位素质量的1/12。

Relative atomic mass/atomic weights: the ratio of actual mass respect to atomic mass unit (the 1/12th of the mass of carbon-12 atom).

相对原子质量/原子量:原子或元素质量与原子质量单位的比值。

Avogadro's number 阿伏伽德罗常数

Molar mass: The mass of substance in one mole of the substance; numerically equal to the formula weight of the substance.

摩尔质量:1摩尔物质的质量,等于物质的分子量。

Mole: the amount of substance that contains as many entities (atoms, molecules, or other particles) as there are atoms in exactly 0.012 kg of pure carbon-12 atoms.

摩尔:定义为物质的量,与0.012克同位素碳-12所含原子数量的粒子集合体的物理量。

> mole 来自拉丁词源,意味着"a mass"一大块的意思。
> 分子"molecule"则来自同一个词,意味着"a small mass"一小块。

Molecule: The smallest particle of an element or compound that can have a stable independent existence.

分子:是一种元素或化合物具有稳定独立存在的最小粒子。

Molecular weight: The mass, in atomic mass units, of one molecule of a nonionic (molecular) substance.

分子量:基于原子质量单位的一个非离子分子物质的质量。

Chemical formula: Combination of symbols that indicates the chemical composition of a substance.

化学式:是一种表示化学物质中原子组成比例的方法。

Formula weight: The mass, in atomic mass units, of one formula unit of a substance. Numerically equal to the mass, in grams, of one mole of the substance.

式量:基于原子质量单位,一个化学式单位的质量。等于每摩尔该物质的克质量。

Simplest formula/empirical formula: The smallest whole-number ratio of atoms present in a compound.

最简式/化学经验式:化合物中原子的最小整数比。

Structural formula: A representation that shows how atoms are connected in a compound.

结构式:用元素符号和短线表示化合物(或单质)分子中原子的排列和结合方式的示意图。

Reaction formula/ reaction equation:反应式

Stoichiometry: Description of the quantitative relationships among elements in compounds (composition stoichiometry) and among substances as they undergo chemical changes (reaction stoichiometry).

化学计算/化学计量/化学计量学:研究化合物中元素以及物质经历化学变化时的定量关系。

Isotope: the different forms of a chemical element, having the same number of protons, but different numbers of neutrons.

同位素:具有相同质子数,不同中子数的同一元素的不同形式。

Allotropes: Different forms of the same element in the same physical state.

同素异形体:同种元素在相同物理状态下的不同形式。

---

allotr-异:allotriploid 异源三倍体、allotriomorphic 异形的、allotriolith 异质结石

---

graphite 石墨、diamond 金刚石、amorphous carbon 无定形碳为碳的几种同素异形体。

glassy carbon 玻碳、carbon nanotube 纳米碳管、graphene 石墨烯

amorphous carbon 无定形碳,amorphous solid 非晶固体,其中 a-表示"无",-morphous表示"形状",如 morphology 形貌/形态学、polymorphous 多形性、isomorphous 同晶。

字母 m 开头的许多单词均与外形、形状有关,如 mode 模式/方式、model 模型/模特儿、modify 使变形/修饰、mould 模型/模具。

an-也可表示"无",如 anhydrous 无水的、anaerobic 无氧的。

> in-也表示"无",如 inorganic 无机物。
> un-也表示"无",如 unfortunately 不幸地。

ball-and-stick molecular model 球棍分子模型
space-filling molecular model 分子空间填充模型

17　化 学 反 应

Chemical equations are used to describe chemical reactions, and they show (1) the substances that react, called reactants; (2) the substances formed, called products; and (3) the relative amounts of the substances involved.

化学方程式用来描述化学反应,表明反应物、产物以及所涉及纯净物的相对数量关系。

Chemical equation: Description of a chemical reaction by placing the formulas of reactants on the left and the formulas of products on the right of an arrow. A chemical equation must be balanced; that is, it must have the same number of each kind of atom on both sides.

化学方程式:是对化学反应的描述,反应物写在箭头的左边,产物在右边。化学方程式必须平衡。也就是说,两边每种元素必须有相同的数目。

Reactions that can occur in both directions are reversible reactions.

在正反两个方向都能发生的反应称之为可逆反应。

A reversible reaction is a chemical reaction where the reactants form products that, in turn, react together to give the reactants back. It finally results in an equilibrium mixture of reactants and products.

可逆反应是一种反应物生成产物、产物又生成反应物的化学反应。最终导致反应物和产物混合物的平衡。

> equal 相等的/平等的/等于、equality 等量、equalization 均分、equilibrium 平衡、equivalent 相等的/当量

Reactants: Substances consumed in a chemical reaction.

反应物:在化学反应中消耗的物质。

Products: Substances produced in a chemical reaction.

产物:化学反应中生成的物质。

Reaction ratio: The relative amounts of reactants and products involved in a reaction; may be the ratio of moles, or masses.

反应比:反应中反应物和产物的相对量,可以是摩尔比,或者质量比。

Theoretical yield: The maximum amount of a specified product that could be obtained from specified amounts of reactants, assuming complete consumption of the limiting reactant according to only one reaction and complete recovery of the product.

理论产量:假定只按照一个反应,完全消耗限制反应物且完全收获产物,从特定量反应物所获得的特定产物的最大数量。

The actual yield is the amount of a specified pure product actually obtained from a given reaction.

实际产量是一个给定反应实际获得的特定产物的数量。

Percent yield: 100% times actual yield divided by theoretical yield.

百分比产量:实际产量除以理论产量,并乘以100%。

1. 氧化还原反应

Oxidation is an increase in oxidation number and corresponds to the loss of electrons.

氧化涉及氧化态的增加和电子的失去。

The oxidation state, often called the oxidation number, is an indicator of the degree of oxidation of an atom in a chemical compound.

氧化态,常常称之为氧化数,表明原子在化合物中的氧化程度。

Oxidizing agent: The substance that oxidizes another substance and is reduced.

氧化剂:能氧化另一个物质而自身被还原的物质。

Reduction is a decrease in oxidation number and corresponds to a gain of electrons.

还原涉及氧化态的下降,符合电子的获得。

> reduction 既表示还原,也有减少、降低的意思,因为还原意味着价态的降低。

oxidation-reduction reaction/redox reactions: the reactions that involve the transfer of electrons from one species to another.

氧化还原反应:涉及电子转移的反应。

> redox 是由 reduction 还原和 oxidation 氧化组合在一起的单词。

A disproportionation reaction is a redox reaction in which the same element is oxidized and reduced.

歧化反应是一种氧化还原反应，同一元素发生氧化作用和还原作用。

Disproportionation reaction: A redox reaction in which the oxidizing agent and the reducing agent are the same element.

歧化反应：氧化剂和还原剂是同一个元素的氧化还原反应。

2. 化合反应

Reactions in which two or more substances combine to form a compound are called <u>combination</u> reactions.

两种或两种以上的物质生成一种新物质的反应称之为化合反应。

3. 分解反应

<u>Decomposition</u> reaction is the separation of a chemical compound into elements or simpler compounds.

分解反应指一种化合物在特定条件下分解成两种或两种以上元素或化合物的反应。

---

degradation reaction: A type of organic chemical reaction in which a compound is converted into a simpler compound.

降解反应：指高分子量的或复杂的物质转化为比较简单的物质的过程。

降解反应对应化学合成 chemical synthesis

---

4. 置换反应

Reactions in which one element displaces another from a compound are called <u>displacement reactions.</u>

置换反应指一种单质和一种化合物生成另一种单质和另一种化合物的反应。

Active metals displace less active metals or hydrogen from their compounds in aqueous solution to form the oxidized form of the more active metal and the reduced (free metal) form of the other metal or hydrogen.

在水溶液中，活泼金属替换化合物中的较不活泼金属或氢形成活泼金属的氧化态或者较不活泼金属和氢的还原态。

5. 复分解反应

<u>Metathesis reactions</u> (or double decomposition reaction, exchange reactions) are reactions in which the products are formed by the exchange of the ions in the two reactants to form two new compounds.

复分解反应是由两种化合物互相交换成分,生成另外两种化合物的反应。

In many reactions between two compounds in aqueous solution, the positive and negative ions appear to "change partners" to form two new compounds, with no change in oxidation numbers. Such reactions are called metathesis reactions.

在许多反应中,水溶液中的两个化合物彼此交换正负离子形成新的化合物,而没有氧化态的变化。这种反应称之为复分解反应。

6. 沉淀反应

<u>Precipitation reactions</u> is a double displacement reaction which occurs when an insoluble solid, a precipitate, forms and then settles out of solution.

沉淀反应是一个复分解反应,发生时一个不溶性的固体或沉淀形成并从液体中析出。

Precipitate: An insoluble solid that forms and separates from a solution.

沉淀:在液体中形成并而分离出来的不溶性固体。

7. 产气反应

Gas-formation reaction is a double displacement reaction that form a gas as one of the products.

产气反应是一个能够形成气体的复分解反应。

Gas-formation reaction: A metathesis reaction in which an insoluble or slightly soluble gas is formed as a product.

产气反应:产物生成不溶或轻微不溶气体的复分解反应。

8. 中和反应

Acid-base (<u>neutralization</u>) reactions are a special type of double displacement reaction which occurs between an acid and a base to form a salt and water.

酸碱中和反应是一种特殊的复分解反应,在酸和碱之间反应生成盐和水。

9. 有机反应

Addition reaction: A reaction in which two atoms or groups of atoms are added to a molecule, one on each side of a double or triple bond. The number of groups attached to carbon increases, and the molecule becomes more nearly saturated.

加成反应：两个原子或者基团加到双键或三键两边的反应。与碳相连的基团越多，分子越接近饱和。

Condensation reaction: A reaction in which a small molecule, such as water or hydrogen chloride, is eliminated and two molecules are joined.

缩合反应：两个分子失去一个水分子或者氯化氢分子而结合的反应。

Elimination reaction: A reaction in which the number of groups attached to carbon decreases. The degree of unsaturation in the molecule increases.

消去反应：与碳相连的基团数减少的反应，分子的不饱和度增加。

Hydration reaction: A reaction in which the elements of water, H and OH, add across a double or triple bond.

水化反应：水的两个成分 H 和 OH 加到双键或三键的两端的反应。

Polymerization: The combination of many small molecules (monomers) to form large molecules (polymers).

聚合：组合许多小分子单体行程聚合物大分子。

Substitution reaction: A reaction in which an atom or a group of atoms attached to a carbon atom is replaced by another atom or group of atoms. No change occurs in the degree of saturation at the reactive carbon.

取代反应：与碳相连的原子或基团被另外的原子或基团替换的反应，该碳原子的饱和度不变。

Stereoisomers: Isomers in which the atoms are linked together in the same atom-to-atom order, but with different arrangements in space.

立体异构体：原子相连顺序相同，但空间排列不同的异构体。

Constitutional isomers: Compounds that contain the same numbers of the same kinds of atoms but that differ in the order in which their atoms are bonded together.

构型异构体：原子种类和数目相同，但原子结合顺序不同的化合物。

Geometric isomers/cis-trans isomer: Compounds with different arrangements of groups on the opposite sides of a bond with restricted rotation, such as a double bond or a single bond in a ring; for example, cis-trans isomers of certain alkenes.

几何异构体/顺反异构体：因双键或成环碳原子的单键不能自由旋转而引起的键对面基团的不同排列的化合物。

Optical isomers/enantiomers: Molecules that are nonsuperimposable mirror images of each other, that is, that bear the same relationship to each other as do left and right hands.

旋光异构体/对应异构体：分子中没有反轴对称性而引起的具有不同旋光性能的分子。

18 原子结构

Atoms consist of very small, very dense positively charged nuclei surrounded by clouds of electrons at relatively great distances from the nuclei.
原子含有极小的、非常致密的正电荷的原子核,被离核较远的电子云所包围。
Atom: The smallest particle of an element that maintains its chemical identity through all chemical and physical changes.
原子:指一个元素能够在化学和物理变化中保持它的化学特性的最小粒子。
Atomic number (Z): The number of protons in the nucleus of an atom.
原子序数:原子核内中子的数目。
An atomic orbital is a region of space in which the probability of finding an electron is high.
原子轨道是电子出现几率高的区域。
Fundamental particles: Subatomic particles of which all matter is composed; protons, electrons, and neutrons are fundamental particles.
基本粒子:构成所有物质的亚原子粒子。质子、电子和中子都是基本粒子。
Alpha particle (α): A particle that consists of two protons and two neutrons; identical to a helium nucleus.
α粒子:由两个质子和两个中子组成的粒子,等于一个氦核。

> electron 电子, proton 质子, neutron 中子:原子主要由电子、质子和中子三种基本粒子所构成。
> 比较上述三个基本粒子的英文名称,可以发现一个共同的词根:
> -on 子:ion 离子、fermion 费米子、soliton 孤子、mesotron 介子、boson 玻色子

Cathode ray: The beam of electrons going from the negative electrode toward the positive electrode in a cathode-ray tube.
阴极射线:在阴极射线管内从负极发往正极的电子束。
Diamagnetism: Weak repulsion by a magnetic field; associated with all electrons being paired.
反磁性:当一些物质处在外加磁场中,对磁场产生的微弱斥力。与成对电子相关。

Paramagnetism: Attraction toward a magnetic field, stronger than diamagnetism, but still very weak compared with ferromagnetism; due to presence of unpaired electrons.

顺磁性：对磁场的吸引力，比反磁性强，比铁磁性弱；是由于不成对电子所引起的。

Ferromagnetism: The property that allows a substance to become permanently magnetized when placed in a magnetic field; exhibited by iron, cobalt, and nickel.

铁磁性：使得物质在磁场作用下变得永久磁化的特性，铁、钴、镍具有该特性。

Electromagnetic radiation: Energy that is propagated by means of electric and magnetic fields that oscillate in directions perpendicular to the direction of travel of the energy.

电磁辐射：是以电场或磁场传播的能量，电场或磁场在垂直于能量传播方向上振荡。

Natural radioactivity: Spontaneous decomposition of an atom.

天然放射性：原子的自发降解。

> 上面涉及的两个词：radiation 辐射和 radio 放射，均有向四周发散的含义。
>
> 字母 r 开头的单词许多和太阳的性质相关，太阳每日循环往复，有轮子、圆、绕、重复、返回等相关含义：
>
>   round 圆形的、roll 滚动、rim 轮缘、rotor 转子、旋翼
>
>   radar 雷达、radial 放射的、radiate 辐射的/发光的、radiation 辐射、radius 半径/范围、range 范围、ray 光线/射线
>
>   repeat 重复、recall 召回、reconstruct 重建、refine 提炼/使高雅、rejuvenate 返老还童、reproduce 复制、resonant 共振的/响亮的、revival 苏醒
>
>   repulse 驳斥、revenge 复仇、reverse 翻转/反转、revolt 反叛

The Heisenberg Uncertainty Principle: It is impossible to determine accurately both the momentum and the position of an electron (or any other very small particle) simultaneously.

海森堡不确定性原理/测不准原理：不可能同时准确测定电子或其他极小粒子的动量和位置。

Pauli Exclusion Principle: No two electrons in an atom may have identical sets of four quantum numbers.

泡利不相容原理：一个原子内部没有两个电子具有同样的 4 个量子数。

Hund's Rule: Electrons occupy all the orbitals of a given subshell singly before pairing begins. These unpaired electrons have parallel spins.

洪特规则：电子成对前的排布必先尽可能分占在同一电子亚层的各个轨道上，且自旋平行。

Electron configuration: The specific distribution of electrons in the atomic orbitals of atoms and ions.

电子构型：原子和离子的原子轨道上电子的分布排列。

Quantum: A "packet" of energy.

量子：一"包"能量。

> 量子一词来自拉丁语 quantus，意为"多少"，代表"相当数量的某事"。
> quantity 数量、quantify 定量

Quantum mechanics: A mathematical method of treating particles on the basis of quantum theory.

量子力学：基于量子理论研究粒子的数学方法。

Quantum numbers: Numbers that describe the energies of electrons in atoms.

量子数：描述原子中电子能量的数字。

The principal quantum number (n) describes the electron shell, or energy level, of an atom.

主量子数描述原子的电子壳层，或者能级。

Angular momentum quantum number/azimuthal quantum number: a quantum number for an atomic orbital that determines its orbital angular momentum and describes the shape of the orbital. It is also known as the orbital angular momentum quantum number, orbital quantum number or second quantum number.

角量子数：确定轨道角动量的原子轨道的数字，它表示轨道的形状。也称之为轨道角动量量子数，轨道量子数或第二量子数。

Magnetic quantum number (m) designates the particular orbital within a given subshell (s, p, d, f) in which an electron resides.

磁量子数表示电子所在亚层内的特定轨道。

Spin quantum number describes the direction in which an electron spins in an orbital.

自旋量子数描述轨道内电子自旋方向。

Ground state: The lowest energy state or most stable state of an atom, molecule, or ion.

基态：原子、分子或离子的最低能量状态，也是最稳定的状态。

Excited state：Any energy state other than the ground state of an atom, ion, or molecule.

激发态：原子、离子或分子基态之外的所有能量状态。

Electron transition：The transfer of an electron from one energy level to another.

电子跃迁：电子从一个能级到另一个能级的跃迁。

> trans-词根对应汉语"穿、传、转"之意，如 transfer 转让、transport 传送、transform 变换、transparent 透明的

Wavelength：The distance between two identical points of a wave.

波长：波两个相同点之间的距离。

Frequency：The number of crests of a wave that pass a given point per unit time.

频率：单位时间通过特定点的波峰数。

> frequently 频繁的

Photoelectric effect：Emission of an electron from the surface of a metal, caused by impinging electromagnetic radiation of certain minimum energy; the resulting current increases with increasing intensity of radiation.

光电效应：施加很小能量的电磁辐射在金属表面引起的电子逸出。

Spectrum：Display of component wavelengths of electromagnetic radiation.

光谱：电磁辐射的构成波长的显示。

> 表示眼睛、看等词汇常常也具有光学、眼镜、检查、聪明、智慧等含义：
> spectrum 光谱、spectacular 壮观的/引人注意的、spectacle 眼镜/奇观、spectra 光谱/范围、mass spectrometer 质谱、spectroscopy 光谱学/能谱法、speculate 推测/思索、inspection 检查、inspectors 检察员
> scope 眼界/审视/仔细研究、scopy 镜检/检查法/观察、microscopy 显微术/显微检查法、spectroscopy 光谱学、radioscopy 放射性检测法
> observe 观察/注意、inobservant 不注意的/疏忽的、unobservant 不注意的/不遵守的
> optic/optical 眼镜的/光学的/镜片、optics 光学

> video 电视/录像、vide 请见/参阅、vision 视力/幻影/想象、visual 视觉的/光学的、visualization 形象化/目测、view 看/风景/看法、viewpoint 观点/意见
>
> veda 吠陀,是婆罗门教和现代的印度教最重要和最根本的经典,意思是"知识"、"启示"。
>
> wisdom 智慧/知识、wise 聪明的/智慧的、wit 机智/智慧、witness 目击证人

> spectrum 光谱,具有连续不同颜色条纹的含义,一个相似的词是 chromatograph/colour spectrum 色谱。
>
> chroma-与 colour 同源,也具有彩色条纹的含义。而 chromatography 色谱最初的含义就是将样品中的不同组分分离并显色。另外元素 chromium 铬也来自同样词源,因为铬的化合物常常呈现出各种鲜艳的色彩。

Emission spectrum: The spectrum associated with emission of electromagnetic radiation by atoms (or other species) resulting from electron transitions from higher to lower energy states.

发射光谱:原子中的电子从高能态返回到低能态时形成的电磁辐射相应的光谱。

Absorption spectrum: The spectrum associated with absorption of electromagnetic radiation by atoms (or other species) resulting from transitions from lower to higher energy states.

吸收光谱:原子或其他物质吸收电磁辐射,从低能态到高能态转换所对应的光谱。

> 注意 absorption 和 adsorption 的区别:
> absorption 吸收、absorptiometry 吸光测定法、absorption coefficient 吸收系数
> absorb 吸收/吸取、absorbance 吸光度
> adsorption 吸附、adsorptive 吸附的
> adsorb 吸附/吸收、adsorber 吸附器/吸收器
> 无论是 adsorb 还是 absorb,后面的-sorb 均来自拉丁语 sorbere,意为吮吸、吸入,其更古老的源头是古印欧语词根 srebh-表示"to suck, absorb"。同源词汇有:
> suck 吮吸/吸、sup 小口喝

19　元素周期律

Periodic law：The properties of the elements are periodic functions of their atomic numbers.
周期率：元素的性质随原子序数周期性变化。
Periodic table：An arrangement of elements in order of increasing atomic number that also emphasizes periodicity.
周期表：根据原子序数的增加顺序和周期型规律对元素的排列。
Period：The elements in a horizontal row of the periodic table.
周期:元素周期表中一横行称之为一周期。
Column/group/family：A vertical column in the periodic table.
族:元素周期表的纵列称之为族。
Alkali metals：Elements of Group IA in the periodic table, except hydrogen.
碱金属：周期表第一主族中除氢以外的元素。
Alkaline earth metals：Group IIA elements in the periodic table.
碱土金属：周期表第二主族元素。

碱有两种表示方法：
alkali 碱、alkalic/alkaline 碱性的、alkaloid 生物碱
base 碱、basic 碱性的

The elements of Group VIIA are known as halogens.
第七主族元素称之为卤素。
Lanthanides elements 镧系元素
Noble/rare/inert gases：Elements of Group VIIIA in the periodic table.
惰性/稀有气体：周期表中第八主族元素。

---
noble/rare 有稀有、珍贵、高贵的意思,所以 noble metal 表示贵金属。
贵金属通常是惰性的,所以也用 noble/rare gases 表示惰性气体。

Noble gas configuration：The stable electron configuration of a noble gas.
稀有气体构型：稀有气体的稳定电子构型。

d-Transition elements: The B group elements in the periodic table.

d 区过渡元素：周期表中的副族元素。

Active metal: A metal that readily loses electrons to form cations.

活泼金属：容易失去电子形成阳离子的金属。

Metals that exhibit variable oxidation states react with a limited amount of oxygen to give oxides with lower oxidation states (such as FeO and Cu_2O). They react with an excess of oxygen to give oxides with higher oxidation states (such as Fe_2O_3 and CuO).

有多种氧化态的金属和有限氧反应生成低氧化态的氧化物，和过量的氧反应生成高价态的氧化物。

Metalloids: Elements with properties intermediated between metals and non-metals: B, Si, Ge, As, Sb, Te, Po, and At.

类金属：性质在金属和非金属之间的元素，如：B、Si、Ge、As、Sb、Te、Po、At。

> -oid，来源于希腊语，意为外表或形状，可译为"……形的、……似的"或"类……、似……"。如：
> anthropoid 似人的/类人猿、trichoid 发状、ichthyoid 鱼形的、dendroid 树状的

Semiconductor: A substance that does not conduct electricity at low temperatures but does so at higher temperatures.

半导体：在低温下不导电而在高温下导电的物质。

Atomic radius: The radius of an atom.

原子半径：原子的半径。

Ionic radius: The radius of an ion.

离子半径：离子的半径。

Effective nuclear charge (Z_{eff}) is the net positive charge experienced by an electron in a multi-electron atom. The term "effective" is used because the shielding effect of negatively charged electrons prevents higher orbital electrons from experiencing the full nuclear charge by the repelling effect of inner-layer electrons.

有效核电荷是多电子原子中一个电子的净电荷。说它"有效"是因为通过芯电子的排斥作用，负电荷电子的屏蔽作用阻止高轨道电子收到核电荷的全部作用。

The electron affinity is defined as the amount of energy released when an electron is added to a neutral atom or molecule in the gaseous state to form a negative ion.

电子亲和能/电子亲和势/电子亲和力定义为一个中性的气态原子获得一电子成为-1价气态离子时所放出的能量。

Electronegativity：A measure of the relative tendency of an atom to attract electrons to itself when chemically combined with another atom.

原子成键结合时对电子的相对吸引能力。

Ionization energy：The amount of energy required to remove the most loosely held electron of an isolated gaseous atom or ion.

电离能：除去单独气态原子或离子最松散结合的电子所需要的能量。

The outermost electrons have the greatest influence on the properties of elements. Adding an electron to an inner d orbital results in less striking changes in properties than adding an electron to an outer s or p orbital.

最外层电子对元素性质有最大的影响。在内层d轨道增加一个电子不如在外层s或者p轨道增加对元素性质影响大。

Within a family (vertical group on the periodic table) of representative elements, atomic radii increase from top to bottom as electrons are added to shells farther from the nucleus.

在周期表中同一族内，随着电子在远离原子核的壳层的增加，从上到下，原子半径随之增大。

As we move from left to right across a period in the periodic table, atomic radii of representative elements decrease as a proton is added to the nucleus and an electron is added to a particular shell.

在周期表同一周期中从左向右，随着核内质子数增加和电子在特定层的增加，原子半径减小。

Metallic character increases from top to bottom and decreases from left to right with respect to position in the periodic table.

在周期表中，从上往下，金属性增强，从左往右，金属性降低。

Elements with low ionization energies (IE) lose electrons easily to form cations.

电离能低的元素容易失去电子成为阳离子。

20 化 学 键

Chemical bonds: Attractive forces that hold atoms together in elements and compounds.

化学键：在单质和化合物中把原子结合到一起的吸引力。

> 注意：在这里 element 不表示元素，而是单质的意思。
> bond 联系/捆绑发音近似汉字"绑"，在半导体行业常表示键合的含义，在化学上常表示"……键"。
> 动词是 bind，联结/捆绑。

Ionic bonding is a type of chemical bond that involves the electrostatic attraction between oppositely charged ions.

离子键是一种涉及相反电荷间静电吸引的化学键。

The farther apart across the periodic table two Group A elements are, the more ionic their bonding will be.

在周期表中，两个主族元素相距越远，越易形成离子键。

When the electronegativity difference between two elements is large, as between a metal and a nonmetal, the elements are likely to form a compound by ionic bonding (transfer of electrons).

两个元素电负性相差较大时，就像一个金属和一个非金属，容易通过离子键形成化合物。

A covalent bond is formed when two atoms share one or more pairs of electrons.

当两个原子共享一个或多个电子时，形成共价键。

Covalent bonding occurs when the electronegativity difference between elements (atoms) is zero or relatively small.

元素间电负性差值为 0 或较小时，形成共价键。

> covalent 由 co-和 valent 构成，前者有"共同"之意，后者表示"价的/化学价的"，显然和单词 value 有关：
> value 价值/价格、valuable 有价值的/贵重的、valueless 无价值的/不值钱的

Bonding pair: A pair of electrons involved in a covalent bond. Also called shared pair.

成键电子对:参与共价键的一对电子,也叫做共享电子对。

Lone pair/unshared pair: A pair of electrons residing on one atom and not shared by other atoms.

孤对电子:为一个原子所有,不被其他原子共享的电子对。

Valence electrons: The s and p electrons in the outermost shell of an atom.

价电子:原子最外层的 s 和 p 电子。

Single bond: A covalent bond resulting from the sharing of two electrons (one pair) between two atoms.

单键:在两个原子之间共享一对电子的共价键。

Double bond: A covalent bond resulting from the sharing of four electrons (two pairs) between two atoms.

双键:在两个原子之间共享两对电子的共价键。

Triple bond: A covalent bond resulting from the sharing of six electrons (three pairs) between two atoms.

三键:在两个原子之间共享三对电子的共价键。

Dipole: Refers to the separation of charge between two covalently bonded atoms.

偶极:指两个共价结合的原子中电荷的分离。

Dipole moment can be defined as the product of magnitude of charges and the distance of separation between the charges.

偶极矩是电荷距离和电荷量的乘积。

---

moment 既有瞬间/时刻的含义,也有力矩的意思:

moment 瞬间/时刻、in a moment 一转眼、for a moment 一会儿、at the moment 此刻

moment 力矩

奇怪的是,瞬间/立刻和力矩有什么关系呢? 原来,moment 来自拉丁语,和动词 move 同源,原意为运动、变化,有瞬时之意,引申出动量的含义,如:

angular momentum 角动量

Nonpolar bond: A covalent bond between two atoms with the same electronegativity, so that the electron density is symmetrically distributed.

非极性键:具有相同电负性的两个原子之间的共价键,电子密度对称分布。

Polar bond: A covalent bond between two atoms with different electrone gativities, so that the electron density is unsymmetrically distributed.

极性键：具有不同电负性的两个原子之间的共价键,电子密度不对称分布。

Central atom: The atom or ion to which the ligands are bonded in a complex species.

中心原子：在配位化合物中,与配体成键的原子或离子。

Chelate: A ligand that utilizes two or more donor atoms in bonding to metals.

螯合剂：利用两个或更多配位原子与金属作用的配体。

Coordination compound or complex: A compound containing coordinate covalent bonds between electron pair donors and a metal.

配位化学物：在电子对供体和金属之间存在配位键的化合物。

21 价键理论

The basic ideas of the valence shell electron pair repulsion (VSEPR) theory are: Each set of valence shell electrons on a central atom is significant. The sets of valence shell electrons on the central atom repel one another. They are arranged about the central atom so that repulsions among them are as small as possible.

价层电子对互斥理论的基本思想是:中心原子的价层电子影响显著。中心原子的价层电子彼此排斥。价层电子排列在中心原子周围使其排斥作用尽可能小。

According to VSEPR theory, the structure is most stable when the regions of high electron density on the central atom are as far apart as possible.

根据价层电子对互斥理论,当中心原子的高电子密度区尽可能远离时,结构最为稳定。

Electron configuration: In atomic physics and quantum chemistry, the electron configuration is the distribution of electrons of an atom or molecule (or other physical structure) in atomic or molecular orbitals.

电子构型/电子组态/电子排序:在原子物理和量子化学中,电子构型是原子或分子在其轨道上的电子分布。

Hybridization: the mixing of atomic orbitals to form new orbitals suitable for bonding.

杂化:混合原子轨道形成新的适合成键的轨道。

> hybridization 杂交/杂化
> hybrid 杂种/混合物、hybrid car 混合动力车、hybrid rice 杂交稻

Lewis formula/Lewis structure/Lewis dot diagram/Lewis dot formulas/Lewis dot structure/electron dot structure are diagrams that show the bonding between atoms of a molecule and the lone pairs of electrons that may exist in the molecule.

路易斯结构式是一种示意图,它描述分子中原子之间的键以及分子中可能存在的孤对电子。

Overlap of orbitals: The interaction of orbitals on different atoms in the same region of space.

轨道的重叠：不同原子在同一空间区域中德轨道相互作用。

Pi (π) bond: A bond resulting from the side-on overlap of atomic orbitals, in which the regions of electron sharing are on opposite sides of and parallel to an imaginary line connecting the bonded atoms.

π 键：由于原子轨道侧向重叠而形成的键，其中电子共享区在成键原子虚拟连接线的两边，且与其平行。

Sigma (σ) bond: A bond resulting from the head-on overlap of atomic orbitals, in which the region of electron sharing is along and (cylindrically) symmetrical to an imaginary line connecting the bonded atoms.

σ 键：由原子轨道头碰头方式形成的键，电子共享区沿连接成键原子虚拟线的两边轴向对称。

Valence bond theory: Assumes that covalent bonds are formed when atomic orbitals on different atoms overlap and electrons are shared.

价键理论：不同原子的原子轨道重叠并且电子共享形成共价键的假说。

Valence shell: The outermost occupied electron shell of an atom.

价电子层：占据原子最外层的电子层。

Bond energy: The amount of energy necessary to break one mole of bonds of a given kind (in the gas phase).

键能：在气相中断裂 1 摩尔键所需要的能量。

Bond order: Half the number of electrons in bonding orbitals minus half the number of electrons in antibonding orbitals.

键级：半数成键轨道电子数减去半数反键轨道电子数。

Bonding orbital: A molecular orbital lower in energy than any of the atomic orbitals from which it is derived; when populated with electrons, lends stability to a molecule or ion.

成键轨道：分子轨道中，能量低于任何其他原子轨道组成的分子轨道，当填入电子时，使得成键的分子或离子稳定。

Nonbonding orbital: A molecular orbital whose occupation by electrons neither increases nor decreases the bond order between the involved atoms.

非键轨道：填入电子既不提高，也不降低参与原子键级的分子轨道。

An antibonding orbital is a form of molecular orbital that is located outside the region of two distinct nuclei. The overlap of the constituent atomic orbitals is said to be out of phase, and as such the electrons present in each antibonding orbital are repulsive and act to destabilize the molecule as a whole.

反键轨道在两个原子核外。组成原子轨道的重叠部分不同相,因此反键轨道中德电子彼此排斥并降低分子的稳定性。

Degenerate orbitals: Orbitals of the same energy.

简并轨道:能量相同的轨道。

Delocalization: The formation of a set of molecular orbitals that extend over more than two atoms; important in species that valence bond theory describes in terms of resonance.

离阈:延展在超过两个原子上的一组分子轨道的形成;在价键理论中用来解释共振时很重要。

Molecular orbital: An orbital resulting from overlap and mixing of atomic orbitals on different atoms. A molecular orbital belongs to the molecule as a whole.

分子轨道:来自于不同原子间原子轨道的重叠和混合形成的轨道。分子轨道属于整个分子。

Nodal plane: A region in which the probability of finding an electron is zero.

波节面:电子出现几率为 0 的区域。

22 气体动力学分子理论

At constant pressure, the volume occupied by a definite mass of a gas is directly proportional to its absolute temperature.

恒压条件下,已知质量的气体所占据的空间与绝对温度成正比。

In 1811, Amedeo Avogadro postulated that at the same temperature and pressure, equal volumes of all gases contain the same number of molecules.

1811年,阿伏伽德罗假设在同温同压下,同样体积的所有气体含有同样数目的分子。

Gay-Lussac's Law of Combining Volumes: At constant temperature and pressure, the volumes of reacting gases can be expressed as a ratio of simple whole numbers.

盖·吕萨克化合体积定律:恒温恒压下,反应气体的体积可以表示为简单的整数比。

> volume 体积/容积/大量的/卷,来自古拉丁语,原意为"卷、书卷"等含义:
> volvox 团藻、vortex 旋风/涡流

Absolute zero: The zero point on the absolute temperature scale; −273.15 ℃ or 0 K; theoretically, the temperature at which molecular motion is a minimum.

绝对零度:绝对温度的0点,等于零下273.15 ℃或者0 K。理论上,在这个温度下,分子运动最低。

Atmosphere (atm): A unit of pressure; the pressure that will support a column of mercury 760 mm high at 0℃.

标准大气压(单位 atm):一个压力单位;在0 ℃支持760 mm汞柱的压力。

> atmosphere 大气/大气层/大气压,其中 atmo- 来自古希腊词源,表示气体、挥发,类似的词还有:
> air 空气
> aero-: aerosol 气溶胶、aerobic 有氧的、aerospace 航空
> sphere 球体/范围/包围,原意有中空、空间之意;spheroid 球状体

Avogadro's Law: At the same temperature and pressure, equal volumes of all gases contain the same number of molecules.

阿伏伽德罗定律：在同温同压下，同等体积的所有气体含有相同数量的分子。

Boyle's Law: At constant temperature, the volume occupied by a given mass of a gas is inversely proportional to the applied pressure.

波义耳定律：在恒温条件下，特定质量的气体体积反比于所施加的压力。

Charles's Law: At constant pressure, the volume occupied by a definite mass of a gas is directly proportional to its absolute temperature.

查理定律：在恒压条件下，特定质量气体占据的体积正比于绝对温度。

Dalton's Law of Partial Pressures: The total pressure exerted by a mixture of gases is the sum of the partial pressures of the individual gases.

道尔顿分压定律：混合气体的总压力等于各部分气体的分压。

Diffusion: The movement of a substance (e. g. , a gas) into a space or the mixing of one substance (e. g. , a gas) with another.

扩散：物质进入空间的运动或者两种物质的混合。

---

diffusion 扩散/弥散，其中 di-表示分离，-fusion 有倾倒/涌流等意。

effusion 流出/喷出，其中 e-表示向外，-fusion 有倾倒/涌流等意。

字母 F 和羽毛形状的相似性使得许多 F 开头或者含有 F 的单词具有浮、轻、像水、火、光一样流出或发射等相关的含义：

fire 发/火、flicker 闪烁、flighty 轻浮的/反复的、float 浮、fly 飞、flight 飞行、flame 火焰、flare 燃烧/发怒、flash 闪耀、flood 洪水、flow 流动、flow injection analysis(FIA)流动进样分析、flowing 流利的、fluent 流利的、fluid 液体/流体、flutter 飘动、fluvial 河流的、fluctuate 波动、foam 泡沫、fog 雾、ford 河流浅水处、fountain 喷泉、froth 泡沫、fume 烟/气、fuse 融化/融合、effuse 流出、effluent 流出的/发射的、infuse 灌输/浸渍

Dispersion Forces: Weak, short-range attractive forces between short-lived temporary dipoles.

色散力：存在于瞬间偶极子之间的弱的、短距离吸引力。

Ideal gas: A hypothetical gas that obeys exactly all postulates of the kinetic-molecular theory.

理想气体：严格遵循分子运动理论学说的假想气体。

> hypothetical 来源于古希雅词汇,和 hypothesis 相同,hypo-表示低于,-thetical/-thesis 与 theory 相同,表示理论/学说,连在一起就是低于理论的,因此是假想的。
>
> hypo-低/次:hypoglycemia 低血糖、hypothermia 低体温、hypodermic 皮下的
>
> hypochlorous acid 次氯酸、sodium hypochlorite 次氯酸钠、sodium hyposulfite/hypo 硫代硫酸钠

Ideal Gas Equation: The product of the pressure and volume of an ideal gas is directly proportional to the number of moles of the gas and the absolute temperature.

理想气体方程:理想气体压力和体积的积正比于气体的摩尔数和绝对温度。

Standard molar volume: The volume occupied by one mole of an ideal gas under standard conditions: 22.414 liters.

标准摩尔体积:标准条件下 1 摩尔理想气体占据的体积是 22.414 升。

23　化学热力学

Thermodynamics: The study of the energy transfers accompanying physical and chemical processes.
热力学/热动力学：研究伴随物理和化学过程的能量转换。
System: The substances of interest in a process.
体系：研究的对象。
Surroundings: Everything in the environment of the system.
环境：体系周围的一切。
Universe: The system plus the surroundings.
宇宙：体系＋环境。
Open system: Both matter and energy are transferred into or out of the system.
敞开系统：与环境之间既有能量传递，也有物质传递。
Closed system: no matter and only energy is transferred into or out of the system.
封闭系统：与环境之间只有能量传递，没有物质传递。
Isolated system: no matter or energy is transferred into or out of the system.
孤立系统：与环境之间既没有能量传递，也没有物质传递。
Internal energy: All forms of energy associated with a specific amount of a substance.
内能：特定量物质的所有形式的能量。
Work: The application of a force through a distance.
功：施加力并作用一段距离。
Calorimeter: A device used to measure the heat transfer that accompanies a physical or chemical change.
量热计：一种装置，测量伴随物理或化学变化的热量转化

> calorimeter 量热计，calori-显然来自热量单位 calory 卡路里。

Isobaric process: the process which occurs at constant pressure.

等压过程:压强始终保持不变的过程。

> isobaric 等压的,其中 iso-表示同,-baric 来自古希腊词源 barys,表示压力、重力,类似词汇如下:
>
> In mass spectrometry, isobaric peptides are the peptides with the same molecular weight or the same mass.
>
> 质谱学中,等重多肽指的是那些分子量或质量相同的多肽。
>
> Isobaric speakers have a speaker design where two drive units are mounted in tandem usually made with subwoofers.
>
> 等压音箱的两个扬声器是串联的超低音音箱。
>
> barometer 气压计,因为早期的气压计是利用水银的重力测量大气压力。
>
> 有趣的是,化学元素 barium 钡也来自同一词源 barys,表示重的意思。
>
> 原来钡元素最早发现于矿物重晶石(barite, barium sulfate, $BaSO_4$)和碳酸钡矿(witherite, barium carbonate, $BaCO_3$),而这两种元素都有较高的比重,其中重晶石常常作为加重剂用在钻井行业中。

Isochoric process: occurs at constant volume (also called isometric/isovolumetric).

等容过程:是在恒量体系的变化过程(又称定容过程)。

Isothermal process: occurs at a constant temperature.

等热过程:是在恒温体系的变化过程。

First Law of Thermodynamics/the Law of Conservation of Energy: The total amount of energy in the universe is constant; energy is neither created nor destroyed in ordinary chemical reactions and physical changes.

热力学第一定律/能量守恒定律:宇宙中能量守恒;在常规化学和物理变化中,能量既不能被创造,也不能被破坏。

Second Law of Thermodynamics: The universe tends toward a state of greater disorder in spontaneous processes.

热力学第二定律:宇宙自发地趋向无序化。

Third Law of Thermodynamics: The entropy of a hypothetical pure, perfect, crystalline substance at absolute zero temperature is zero.

热力学第三定律:在绝对零度时,理想的纯粹、完美晶体的熵为零。

State function: A variable that defines the state of a system; a function that is independent of the pathway by which a process occurs.

状态函数：定义系统状态的参数；独立于过程发生途径的函数。

> function 函数/应变量，a function of 常用来表示随着……而变化：
> Investment is a function of the interest rate.
> 投资随着利率的变化而变。
> The figure shows the current through a 1.5 Ω resistor as a function of time.
> 图表明电流通过 1.5 Ω 电阻时，随着时间的变化。

> variable 变量/多变的，类似单词有"变"、"多"之意：
> variability 变化无常、variable 变量、variance 矛盾/不同、various 各种各样的/不同的、vary 改变/使多样化、vast 巨大的、vastness 巨大/广漠、versatile 多方面的/通用的、versatility 多功能、very 非常
> 相关词汇如：
> parameter 参数、factor 因素/因子/要素

The quantity of heat transferred into or out of a system as it undergoes a chemical or physical change at constant temperature and pressure is defigned the enthalpy change, ΔH.

焓变定义为恒温恒压条件下化学或物理变化所产生的热量变化。

> enthalpy 焓/热含量，其中前缀 en-表示"进入、使……"，-thalpy 来自古希腊词源 thalpein，表示"加热"的意思，类似的词有：
> thermo 热、thermal 热/热的、thermometer 温度计、thermodynamics 热力学

Standard enthalpy change, ΔH^0: The enthalpy change in which the number of moles of reactants specified in the balanced chemical equation, all at standard states, is converted completely to the specified number of moles of products, all at standard states.

标准焓变：根据平衡化学反应式，对应的标准状态的反应物摩尔数全部转换为相应数量的标准状态产物，此过程涉及的焓变。

The standard molar enthalpy of formation, ΔH_f^0, of a substance is the enthalpy change for the reaction in which one mole of the substance in a specified state is formed from its elements in their standard states.

物质的标准摩尔生成焓是从标准状态的元素反应生成 1 摩尔特定状态的物质所引起的焓变。

Hess's Law/the Law of Additivity of rection heat: The enthalpy change for a reaction is the same whether it occurs in one step or a series of steps.

盖斯定律/反应热加成定律：对一个反应而言，无论是通过一步，还是多步进行，其焓变相同。

Entropy, S: A thermodynamic state property that measures the degree of disorder or randomness of a system.

熵：测量系统无序或随机性的热动力学状态性质。

Absolute entropy: The entropy of a substance relative to its entropy in a perfectly ordered crystalline form at 0 K where its entropy is zero.

绝对熵：绝对零度时，物质在完美有序晶体时熵为零，以此为基准，物质的熵。

Gibbs free energy, G: The thermodynamic state function of a system that indicates the amount of energy available for the system to do useful work at constant T and P.

吉布斯自由能：表明可用于系统在恒温恒压下做有用功的热动力学状态函数。

24 化学动力学

Chemical kinetics: The study of rates and mechanisms of chemical reactions and of the factors on which they depend.
化学动力学：研究化学反应速率和机理，及化学反应影响因素。
Thermodynamically favorable (spontaneous) reaction: A reaction that occurs with a net release of free energy.
热动力学有利反应：释放自由能的反应。
Activation energy: The kinetic energy that reactant molecules must have to allow them to reach the transition state so that a reaction can occur.
活化能：反应物分子发生化学反应要达到活跃状态所需要的能量。
Effective collision: A collision between molecules that results in reaction; one in which molecules collide with proper orientations and with sufficient energy to react.
有效碰撞：导致反应的分子之间的碰撞；以合适的定向和足够的能量，导致反应的分子碰撞。
Transition state: A relatively high-energy state in which bonds in reactant molecules are partially broken and new ones are partially formed.
过渡态：一个相对能量较高的状态，反应物分子之间的键部分断裂，新键部分形成。
Reaction intermediate: A species that is produced and then entirely consumed during a multistep reaction; usually shortlived.
反应中间体：在多步反应中生成并完全消耗的物质，通常寿命较短。
Half-life of a reactant: The time required for half of that reactant to be converted into product.
反应物半衰期：半数反应物转化为产物所需要的时间。
Rate of reaction: The change in concentration of a reactant or product per unit time.
反应速率：单位时间反应物或产物浓度的变化。
Rate-determining step: The slowest step in a reaction mechanism; the step that limits the overall rate of reaction.

速度控制步骤：反应机理中最慢的步骤；限制整个反应速率的步骤。

Catalyst：A substance that increases the rate at which a reaction occurs. It remains unchanged when the reaction is complete.

催化剂：加快反应速率的物质，当反应完成时自身不变。

Heterogeneous catalyst：A catalyst that exists in a different phase (solid, liquid, or gas) from the reactants.

异相催化剂：与反应物在不同相中的催化剂。

Homogeneous catalyst：A catalyst that exists in the same phase (liquid or gas) as the reactants.

同相催化剂：与反应物在同相中的催化剂。

Enzyme：A protein that acts as a catalyst in a biological system.

酶：在生物系统中作为催化剂的蛋白质。

Substrate：A reactant in an enzyme-catalyzed reaction.

底物：酶催化反应中的反应物。

substrate 底物/底层/基底/基层

25　气体、液体和固体

The partial pressure of vapor molecules above the surface of a liquid at equilibrium at a given temperature is the vapor pressure of the liquid at that temperature. Because the rate of evaporation increases with increasing temperature, vapor pressures of liquids always increase as temperature increases.

特定温度下液体表面达到平衡时其表面蒸汽分子的分压称之为该液体在此温度下的蒸汽压。因为蒸发的速率随着温度的上升而增大,液体的蒸汽压总是随着温度的增加而增加。

Boiling point: The temperature at which the vapor pressure of a liquid is equal to the external pressure.

沸点:液体的蒸汽压和外部压力相等时的温度。

Band: A series of very closely spaced, nearly continuous molecular orbitals that belong to the crystal as a whole.

能带:属于整个晶体的一系列非常接近的,几乎连续的分子轨道。

Band gap: An energy separation between an insulator's highest filled electron energy band and the next higher-energy vacant band.

带隙:绝缘体填充电子的最高能带和相邻最高能量的空带之间的能量差。

The conduction band is the range of electron energies enough to free an electron from binding with its atom to move freely within the atomic lattice of the material as a'delocalized electron.

导带是一段电子能量范围,它足以释放原子结合的电子,使之成为离阈化电子在材料的原子晶格中自由移动。

Coordination number: In describing crystals, the number of nearest neighbors of an atom or ion.

配位数:晶体中,一个原子或离子紧邻原子的数目。

Crystal lattice: The pattern of arrangement of particles in a crystal.

晶格:晶体中粒子的排列模式。

Crystalline solid: A solid characterized by a regular, ordered arrangement of particles.

结晶固体:粒子成规则性有序排列的固体。

Unit cell: The smallest repeating unit showing all the structural characteristics of a crystal.

晶胞：体现晶体结构型特征的最小重复单元。

> cell 原意为"小房间"，后来衍生出很多类似的含义：
> cell 细胞/电池/小室
> 另一个相似来源的词根是：
> cyto-细胞：cytochrome 细胞色素、cytoplasm 细胞质、cytotoxicity 细胞毒性

> unit 单位/单元，字母 u 构成的很多词汇都有全部、整体、单、一的含义，也许是字母 U 的形状像容器，具有包含的意味：
> ubiquitous 无处不在的、unanimity 全体一致、unicellular 单细胞的、unicorn 独角兽、unicycle 独轮车、uniform 统一标准的、unify 统一、unlateral 单边的、union 联合、unit 单元、unique 独特的、unisex 不分男女的、universal 普遍的/一致的、universe 宇宙/世界/万物、university 综合性大学、utter 说/完全的

Amorphous solid: A noncrystalline solid with no well-defined, ordered structure.

非晶固体：没有有序结构的非晶固体。

Polymorphous: Refers to substances that crystallize in more than one crystalline arrangement.

多形性：以不止一种晶体排列结晶的物质。

Isomorphous: Refers to crystals having the same atomic arrangement.

同晶：相同原子排列的晶体。

> isomorphous 同晶，其中 iso-表示"同"，-morphous 表示"形状"。

Metallic bonding: Bonding within metals due to the electrical attraction of positively charged metal ions for mobile electrons that belong to the crystal as a whole.

金属键：在金属内部，正电荷金属离子对属于整个晶体共有化电子的吸引作用所形成的键。

Alloying: Mixing of a metal with other metals to modify its properties.

合金：将别的金属和一种金属混合以改变其特性。

Semiconductor: A substance that does not conduct electricity well at low temperatures but that does at higher temperatures.

半导体：在低温下导电差，在高温下导电好的物质。

Insulator: A poor conductor of electricity and heat.

绝缘体/隔热体：对电和热传导不好的物质。

Distillation: The separation of a liquid mixture into its components on the basis of differences in boiling points.

蒸馏：基于沸点差异从液体混合物分离其成分。

Evaporation: Vaporization of a liquid below its boiling point.

挥发：液体低于沸点的气化。

Sublimation: The direct vaporization of a solid by heating without passing through the liquid state.

升华：不经过液化阶段，通过加热使固体直接蒸发。

Deposition: The direct solidification of a vapor by cooling; the reverse of sublimation.

沉积：通过冷却直接固化气体，与升华相反。

Condensation: Liquefaction of vapor.

冷凝：气体的液化。

Condensed phases: The liquid and solid phases; phases in which particles interact strongly.

凝聚态：液态和固态；粒子作用较强的相态。

> condense 意为 make dense，"使……致密"的意思。
> dense 致密/厚的、density 密度

Critical temperature: The temperature above which a gas cannot be liquefied.

临界温度：液体能维持液相的最高温度。

Heat of fusion: The amount of heat required to melt a specific amount of a solid at its melting point with no change in temperature.

融化热：在熔点融化特定量的固体而温度不变所需要的热量。

Phase diagram: A diagram that shows equilibrium temperature-pressure relationships for different phases of a substance.

相图/相态图：表明不同相物质的温度—压力平衡关系的图。

> diagram 图，其中 dia-表示"画叉、做记号"，-gram 来自 graphein，与 graphite 石墨同源，表示"写、画"等含义。
> dia-通过/横过：diameter 直径、diathermy 透热法、dielectric 电介质/电介体

Intermolecular forces: Forces between individual particles (atoms, molecules, ions) of a substance.

分子间作用力：物质个体粒子如原子、分子和离子之间的作用力。

Intramolecular forces: Forces between atoms (or ions) within molecules (or formula units).

分子内作用力：在分子内部原子或离子之间的作用力。

Dispersion forces: Very weak and very short-range attractive forces between short-lived temporary (induced) dipoles; also called London forces.

色散力：在寿命较短的暂态偶极子之间的非常弱、且短程的吸引力。

A hydrogen bond is the electromagnetic attractive interaction between polar molecules, in which hydrogen (H) is bound to a highly electronegative atom, such as nitrogen (N), oxygen (O) or fluorine (F).

氢键是一种极性分子之间的电磁吸引力，其中氢与高电负性的原子如氮、氧、氟相结合。

Adhesive force: Force of attraction between a liquid and another surface.

附着力：液体和另一个表面之间的吸引力。

Cohesive forces: All the forces of attraction among particles of a liquid.

内聚力/黏结力：液体粒子之间的所有力。

Surface tension is a contractive tendency of the surface of a liquid that allows it to resist an external force.

表面张力是液体表面抵抗外部力量的收缩性趋势。

Capillary action: The drawing of a liquid up the inside of a smallbore tube when adhesive forces exceed cohesive forces.

毛细作用：在小截面管子内部，当附着力大于内聚力时，液体向上的提升。

Viscosity: The tendency of a liquid to resist flow.

黏性/黏度：液体抵抗流动的趋势。

A supercritical fluid is any substance at a temperature and pressure above its critical point, where distinct liquid and gas phases do not exist. It can effuse through solids like a gas, and dissolve materials like a liquid. In addition, close to the critical point, small changes in pressure or temperature result in large changes in density and many properties.

超临界流体是温度及压力均处于临界点以上的物质，此时液体与气体分界消失。它可以像气体一样穿过固体，像液体一样溶解材料。此外，接近临界点时，压力或温度的微小变化会导致密度和许多性质的巨变。

26 分 散 体 系

A <u>dispersion</u> is a system in which particles are dispersed in a continuous phase of a different composition (or state).

分散系是一个系统中粒子在另一个不同成分的连续相中的分散。

1. 溶液

A <u>solution</u> is a <u>homogeneous</u> mixture, at the molecular level, of two or more substances.

溶液是两种或多种物质在分子水平上的均相混合物。

Simple solutions usually consist of one substance, the <u>solute</u>, dissolved in another substance, the <u>solvent</u>. Aqueous solutions are usually used in laboratory.

简单的溶液通常由一种溶质溶解在另一种溶剂中。实验室常用到水溶液。

<u>Concentrations</u> of solutions are expressed in terms of either the amount of solute present in a given mass or volume of solution, or the amount of solute dissolved in a given mass or volume of solvent.

溶液浓度可以表示为在给定溶液或溶剂重量或体积中溶质的含量。

When we <u>dilute</u> a solution by mixing it with more solvent, the amount of solute present does not change.

当我们通过加入混合更多溶剂来稀释溶液时,溶质的量不变。

2. 胶体

<u>Colloidal</u> system or colloidal dispersion is a heterogeneous system in which very small particles are microscopically dispersed in a continuous phase of a different composition.

胶体系统或胶体分散是一个非匀相系统,其中微小的粒子在不同成分的连续相中显微分散。

The colloidal dispersion is relatively stable since these particles are small enough to be influenced by thermal fluctuations and not be dominated by gravity.

胶体系统具有相对稳定性,主要是粒子足够小,能够被热扰动影响,以至于可以忽略重力的影响。

Usually, the dispersed particles have a diameter of between approximately 1 and 1 000 nanometers.

通常,这些分散粒子的直径大约在 1 到 1 000 nm 之间。

The colloidal dispersion shows the Tyndall effect, which is the scattering of light by particles in the colloid.

由于光在粒子表面的散射,胶体分散呈现丁达尔效应。

Dispersed phase: The solute-like species in a colloid.

分散相:胶体中类似溶质的成分。

Dispersing medium: The solvent-like phase in a colloid.

分散介质:胶体中类似溶剂的相。

hydrophilic colloids 亲水性胶体、hydrophobic colloids 疏水性胶体

3. 溶胶

A sol is a colloidal suspension of very small solid particles in a continuous liquid medium.

溶胶是微小固体粒子在连续液相中的胶体分散。

4. 气溶胶

An aerosol is a colloid of fine solid particles or liquid droplets in gas. Examples of aerosols include haze, dust and smoke.

气溶胶是微小固体或液体粒子在气相中的分散。粒子包括烟雾、灰尘和烟。

5. 固溶胶

A solid sol is a colloid where the continuous phase and the disperse phase are solids. An example of a solid sol is a pearl.

固溶胶是一种胶体,其中连续相和分散相都是固体,比如珍珠。

6. 悬浊液

A turbid liquid is a dispersion of large solid particles in a continuous liquid medium. An example is turbid water of Yellow River.

悬浊液是大的固体粒子在液体介质中的分散,如浑浊的黄河水。

7. 乳液

An <u>emulsion</u> is a dispersion of two or more liquids that are normally immiscible (nonmixable or unblendable).

乳液是两个或多个不互溶液体的分散,比如牛奶。

8. 胶束

A <u>micelle</u> or <u>micella</u> is an aggregate of surfactant molecules dispersed in a liquid where these molecules are assembled with their hydrophobic tails directed toward the center and their hydrophilic heads directed outward.

胶束是表面活性分子在液体中分散的团聚体,这些分子以疏水端向内,亲水端向外的方式组装。

Emulsifying agent/emulsifier: A substance that coats the particles of a dispersed phase and prevents coagulation of colloidal particles.

乳化剂:覆盖分散相粒子阻止其团聚的物质。

A <u>detergent</u> is a surfactant or a mixture of surfactants with cleaning properties in dilute solutions.

洗涤剂是混合表面活性剂,在稀溶液中具有清洁特性。

Surfactant/surface-active agent: a substance that has the ability to emulsify and wash away oil and grease in an aqueous suspension.

表面活性剂:能够在水悬浮液中乳化并洗去油脂的物质。

> Triton 曲拉通是一种表面活性剂,常用于配制缓冲液。该词原意为希腊神话中人身鱼尾的海神,也表示海王星。

27 水溶液与酸碱盐

Solute：The dispersed (dissolved) phase of a solution.
溶质：溶液中的被分散相。
Solvent：The dispersing medium of a solution.
溶剂：溶液中的分散介质。
Saturated solution：A solution in which no more solute will dissolve at a given temperature.
饱和溶液：特定温度下不能再溶解溶质的溶液。
The statement "like dissolves like" means that polar solvents dissolve ionic and polar molecular solutes, and nonpolar solvents dissolve nonpolar molecular liquids.
相似相溶的说法说明极性溶剂溶解离子化和极性分子溶质,非极性溶剂溶解非极性分子液体。
Hard water：Water containing Fe^{3+}, Ca^{2+}, or Mg^{2+} ions, which form precipitates with soaps.
硬水：含有铁、钙、镁离子的水,能和肥皂形成沉淀。
Heat of solution：The amount of heat absorbed in the formation of a solution that contains one mole of solute; the value is positive if heat is absorbed (endothermic) and negative if heat is released (exothermic).
溶解热：形成含有1摩尔溶质的溶液所吸收的热量;如果该值为正,则是吸热的,如果为负,则放热。
Osmosis：The process by which solvent molecules pass through a semipermeable membrane from a dilute solution into a more concentrated solution.
渗透：溶剂分子通过半透膜从稀溶液进入较浓溶液的过程。
Osmotic pressure：The hydrostatic pressure produced on the surface of a semipermeable membrane by osmosis.
渗透压：在半透膜表面由渗透压产生的静液压。
Reverse osmosis：The forced flow of solvent molecules through a semipermeable membrane from a concentrated solution into a dilute solution.
反向渗透：强迫溶剂分子通过半透膜从浓溶液进入稀溶液。

Electrolyte: A substance whose aqueous solutions conduct electricity.

电解质：水溶液导电的物质。

<u>Ionization</u> refers to the process in which a molecular compound separates or reacts with water to form ions in solution.

电离指分子化合物在溶液中解离或与水分子作用的过程。

<u>Dissociation</u> refers to the process in which a solid ionic compound, such as NaCl, separates into its ions in solution.

解离指固体离子化合物,如 NaCl 在溶液中分解成离子的过程。

Electrolytes are substances whose aqueous solutions conduct electric current. Electric current is carried through aqueous solution by the movement of ions.

电解质是其水溶液导电的物质。离子的运动使得水溶液导电。

Strong acids, strong bases, and most soluble salts are completely or nearly completely ionized (or dissociated) in dilute aqueous solutions, and therefore are strong electrolytes.

强酸、强碱和大多数盐在稀溶溶中完全或几乎完全电离,是强电解质。

An acid can be defined as a substance that produces hydrogen ions, H^+, in aqueous solutions.

酸可以定义为在水溶液中产生氢离子的物质。

The Arrhenius Theory: an acid is a substance that dissociates in water to form hydrogen ions (H^+) in aqueous solution. A base is a substance that dissociates in water to form hydroxide (OH^-) ions in aqueous solution.

阿伦尼乌斯理论：酸是能在水溶液中解离出氢离子的物质。碱是能在水溶液中解离出氢氧根离子的物质。

The Bronsted-Lowry Theory: An acid "donates" hydrogen ions (H^+), otherwise known as protons, to bases, which "accept" them.

布朗斯特和劳里理论：酸给出氢离子或质子,碱接受质子。

The Lewis Theory: An acid is any species that can accept a share in an electron pair. A base is any species that can make available, or "donate", a share in an electron pair.

路易斯理论：酸是能接受电子对的物质,碱式能给出电子对的物质。

Strong acids ionize completely, or very nearly completely, in dilute aqueous solution.

强酸在稀溶液中完全或几乎完全电离。

强酸						
HCl	HBr	HI	HNO$_3$	HClO$_4$	HClO$_3$	H$_2$SO$_4$
Hydrochloric acid	Hydrobromic acid	Hydroiodic acid	Nitric acid	Perchloric acid	Chloric acid	Sulfuric acid

Weak acids ionize only slightly (usually less than 5%) in dilute aqueous solution.

弱酸在稀溶液中仅仅轻微电离,通常小于5%。

典型弱酸:acetic acid 醋酸、phosphoric acid 磷酸

Binary acid 二元酸、ternary acid 三元酸

Acid strengths of most ternary acids containing the same central element increase with increasing oxidation state of the central element and with increasing numbers of oxygen atoms.

大多数含有相同中心元素的三元酸酸强度随着中心元素氧化态和氧原子数的增加而增加。

For most ternary acids containing different elements in the same oxidation state from the same group in the periodic table, acid strengths increase with increasing electronegativity of the central element.

对于含有周期表中同一族不同元素,但氧化态相同的三元酸而言,酸的强度随着中心元素的电负性而增强。

Organic acids contain the carboxylate group of atoms, —COOH. Most common organic acids are weak and can ionize slightly by breaking the O—H bond.

有机酸含有羧基官能团。多数有机酸是弱酸,通过断裂 O—H 键轻微电离。

天然有机酸:tartaric acid 酒石酸、lactic acid 乳酸、formic acid 叶酸。

A base is a substance that produces hydroxide ions, OH$^-$, in aqueous solutions. Strong bases are soluble in water and are dissociated completely in dilute aqueous solution.

碱是在水溶液中产生氢氧根离子的物质。强碱溶于水,在稀溶液中完全解离。

强碱:lithium hydroxide 氢氧化锂 LiOH、sodium hydroxide 氢氧化钠 NaOH、potassium hydroxide 氢氧化钾 KOH、calcium hydroxide 氢氧化钙 Ca(OH)$_2$、barium hydroxide 氢氧化钡 Ba(OH)$_2$

Some metals form ionic hydroxides, but these are so sparingly soluble in water that they cannot produce strongly basic solutions. Typical examples include Cu(OH)$_2$, Zn(OH)$_2$, Fe(OH)$_2$, Fe(OH)$_3$.

有些金属形成离子化氢氧化物,但很难溶于水,无法生成强碱溶液。典型的例

子包括 $Cu(OH)_2$、$Zn(OH)_2$、$Fe(OH)_2$ 和 $Fe(OH)_3$。

Common <u>weak bases</u> are molecular substances that are soluble in water but form only low concentrations of ions in solution. The most common weak base is ammonia, NH_3.

弱碱通常是分子物质,它们溶于水但仅形成低浓度的离子,如氨 NH_3。

A salt is a compound that contains a cation other than H^+ and an anion other than hydroxide ion, OH^-, or oxide ion, O_2^-.

盐是含有除 H^+ 之外的<u>阳离子</u>和除 OH^-、O_2^- 之外的<u>阴离子</u>。

Neutralization: The reaction of an acid with a base to form asalt and water.

中和:酸碱反应生成<u>盐</u>和水。

Ion product for water: An equilibrium constant for the ionization of water.

水的离子积:水的电离平衡常数。

Ionization constant: An equilibrium constant for the ionization of a weak electrolyte.

电离常数:弱电解质的电离平衡常数。

Buffer solution: A solution that resists changes in pH when strong acids or strong bases are added. A buffer solution contains an acid and its conjugate base, so it can react with added base or acid.

缓冲液:能够抵抗强酸强碱对 pH 影响的溶液。缓冲液含有酸和它的共轭碱,所以它能和加入的酸或碱反应。

When a solution of a weak electrolyte is altered by adding one of its ions from another source, the ionization of the weak electrolyte is suppressed. This behavior is termed the <u>common ion effect</u>.

在弱电解质中加入其不同盐来源的同种离子,其电离被抑制,这种行为称之为同离子效应。

Indicator: An organic compound that exhibits different colors in solutions of different acidities; used to indicate the point at which reaction between an acid and a base is complete.

指示剂:根据酸度显示不同颜色的有机化合物,用于指示酸碱反应终点。

Titration: A procedure in which one solution is added to another solution until the chemical reaction between the two solutes is complete; usually the concentration of one solution is known and that of the other is unknown.

滴定:一个溶液滴加到另一个溶液中直至两个溶质反应完全的过程;通常已知一种溶液浓度,测定另外一种。

28　电　化　学

Electrochemistry: The study of the chemical changes produced by electric current and the production of electricity by chemical reactions, where some techniques are developed such as electroanalysis, electrodeposition, electrodegradation, anticorrosion, and electroplating etc.

电化学：研究电与化学反应之间的相互转换，基于电化学，发展了电分析、电沉积、电降解、防腐蚀和电镀等技术。

注意 anode 是阳极，但 anion 却变成了阴离子；cathode 是阴极，但 cation 是阳离子。

另外，容易混淆的是 anode 阳极、cathode 阴极、positive 正极、negative 负极。在电解池中，阳极也是正极，阴极就是负极；而在原电池中，阳极却是负极，阴极是正极。听起来很绕口，其实只要掌握它们最基本的定义就很容易分清了。

Anode: The electrode at which oxidation occurs.
阳极：发生氧化反应的电极。
Cathode: The electrode at which reduction occurs.
阴极：发生还原反应的电极。
Positive electrode: The electrode with higher potential.
正极：处于较高电位的电极。
Negative electrode: The electrode with lower potential.
负极：处于较低电位的电极。

> -od 常用来表示棒状、针状物体的头端，所以称之为"极"，如：
> rod 杆/棒、tripod 三脚架
> optode 光纤探头、electrode 电极、anode 阳极、cathode 阴极、antipodes 地球上相对应的两个地区、diode 二极管

The <u>working electrode</u> is the electrode in an electroanalytical system on which the reaction of interest is occurring. Common working electrodes can consist of inert materials such as gold, silver, platinum, glassy carbon, pyrolytic carbon, and mercury drop and film electrodes. <u>Chemically modified electrodes</u> are employed for the analysis of both organic molecules as well as metal ions.

工作电极是电分析系统中要研究的反应发生所在电极。通常工作电极由惰性材料组成,如金、银、铂、玻碳、热解碳、滴汞和汞膜电极。化学修饰电极常用于有机分子和金属离子的分析。

Ultramicroelectrode（UME）超微电极、rotating disk electrode（RDE）旋转圆盘电极、hanging mercury drop electrode（HMDE）悬汞电极、dropping mercury electrode（DME）滴汞电极

Auxiliary electrode/counter electrode 辅助电极/对电极、reference electrode 参比电极、standard hydrogen electrode（SHE）标准氢电极

Salt bridge：A U-shaped tube containing an electrolyte that connects two half-cells of a voltaic cell.

盐桥:连接伏打电池的两个半电池,充满电解质的 U 形管。

Potential 电压、voltage(V)电压/伏特

Potentials versus the standard hydrogen electrode/Potentials vs. the standard hydrogen electrode

相对标准氢电极的电位

Current 电流、ampere(A)安培

Charge 电荷、coulomb(C)库伦

Faraday：An amount of charge equal to 96 485 coulombs; corresponds to the charge on one mole of electrons.

法拉第:1 摩尔电子所带的电量,等于 96 485 库伦。

Galvanic cell 原电池/伽伐尼电池,也叫 voltaic cell 伏打电池。

Nickel-cadmium cell 镍镉电池、dry cell 干电池、Fuel cell 燃料电池

Concentration cell：A voltaic cell in which the two half-cells are composed of the same species but contain different ion concentrations.

浓差电池:两个半电池含有不同浓度的同一物质的伏打电池。

Primary voltaic cell：A voltaic cell that cannot be recharged; no further chemical reaction is possible once the reactants are consumed.

原电池:不可以充电的伏打电池;一旦反应物消耗完不可能再有化学反应。

Secondary voltaic cell：A voltaic cell that can be recharged; the original reactants can be regenerated by reversing the direction of current flow.

二次电池:可充电的伏打电池;通过改变电流方向可以使得原来的反应物再生。

Sacrificial anode：A more active metal that is attached to a less active metal to protect the less active metal cathode against corrosion.

牺牲阳极：为了保护某金属免于腐蚀，可将一更为活泼的金属附着其上。

Electrolytic cell：An electrochemical cell in which electrical energy causes nonspontaneous redox reactions to occur.

电解池：电能引起非自发氧化还原反应发生的电化学池。

Electroplating：Plating a metal onto a (cathodic) surface by electrolysis.

电镀：通过电解，将某金属镀到一个表面上。

Faraday's Law of Electrolysis：The amount of substance that undergoes oxidation or reduction at each electrode during electrolysis is directly proportional to the amount of electricity that passes through the cell.

法拉第电解定律：电解过程中电极上经历氧化还原物质的量与通过电解池的电量成正比。

Nernst equation：An equation that corrects standard electrode potentials for nonstandard conditions.

能斯特等式：用于计算非标准条件下的标准电极电位的方程式。

Polarization of an electrode：Buildup of a product of oxidation or reduction at an electrode, preventing further reaction.

电极极化：氧化或还原产物在电极表面的堆积影响电极的进一步反应。

29 大型仪器

1. morphological analysis 形貌分析

> morphology 形貌学/形态学
> morph 变形/变种、morphogenesis 形态发生
> mode 模式/状况、model 模型/模特、modify 修饰/使变形

Microscopy is the technical field of using microscopes to view samples and objects that cannot be seen with the unaided eye (objects that are not within the resolution range of the normal eye). There are three well-known branches of microscopy: optical, electron, and scanning probe microscopy.

显微成像是用显微镜看一些肉眼无法看到的样品的技术领域。一般有三个著名的分支:光学显微镜、电子显微镜和扫描探针显微镜。

(1) electron microscopy 电子显微镜
Transmission electron microscope (TEM) 透射电镜
Scanning electron microscope (SEM) 扫描电镜
Scanning transmission electron microscope (STEM) 扫描透射式显微镜
Scanning confocal electron microscopy 扫描共聚焦电子显微镜
(2) scanning probe microscope 扫描探针显微镜
Atomic force microscope (AFM) 原子力显微镜
Scanning tunneling microscope (STM) 扫描隧道显微镜
Photonic force microscope (PFM) 光子力显微镜
Electrochemical scanning microscopy (ESM) 电化学扫描显微镜

2. Spectroscopy 光谱学/光谱分析技术

Spectroscopy measures the interaction of the molecules with electromagnetic radiation. Spectroscopy consists of many different applications such as atomic absorption spectroscopy, atomic emission spectroscopy, ultraviolet-visible spectroscopy, X-ray fluorescence spectroscopy, infrared spectroscopy, Raman spectroscopy, nuclear magnetic resonance spectroscopy, photoemission spectroscopy, Mössbauer spectroscopy and so on.

光谱分析技术测量分子和电磁辐射之间的作用。它有很多不同的应用，如原子吸收光谱、原子发射光谱、紫外可见光谱、X 射线荧光光谱、红外光谱、拉曼光谱、核磁共振光谱、光电光谱、穆斯堡尔光谱等等。

> resonance 共振，其中 re 表示重复/反复，sonance 表示声波/振动：
> sonar 声呐、sonic 声音的/声波的、sonator 声波发生器、sonata 奏鸣曲
> 其实 sing 唱歌、song 歌，也都和声音有关。

3. Mass spectrometry 质谱学/质谱分析

Mass spectrometry measures mass-to-charge ratio of molecules using electric and magnetic fields. There are several ionization methods: electron ionization, chemical ionization, electrospray, fast atom bombardment, matrix-assisted laser desorption/ionization, and others.

质谱分析使用电场和磁场测量分子的质荷比。有几种离子化方法：电子离子化、化学离子化、电喷雾、快原子轰击和基质辅助激光解吸/电离以及其他。

4. Crystallography 结晶学/晶体学/晶体衍射

Crystallography is a technique that characterizes the chemical structure of materials at the atomic level by analyzing the diffraction patterns of electromagnetic radiation. X-rays are most commonly used. From the raw data the relative placement of atoms in space may be determined.

晶体衍射是通过分析电磁辐射的衍射模式，在原子水平表征材料结构的技术。通常用 X 射线。从原始数据中可以检测出原子在空间中的相对位置。

> crystal 晶体、quartz crystal microbalance 石英晶体微天平、crystalline 水晶的、crystal clear 完全透明的/晶莹剔透的、crystallize 结晶
> crystal 来源古印欧语词根，具有冰、透明、结霜、结冰、变硬等含义，与 crust 外壳/结痂同源。

5. Electrochemical analysis 电化学分析

Electroanalytical methods measure the electric signals in an electrochemical cell containing the analyte. The three main categories are potentiometry, coulometry, and voltammetry.

电分析方法测量电化学池中待测物的电信号。三个主要的类别是电位测量、电量测量和伏安测量。

polarograph 极谱仪、voltammerter 伏安仪 、automatic titrator 自动滴定仪、conductivity meter 电导仪 、pH meter pH 计

6. Calorimetry/Thermal analysis 量热法/热分析

Calorimetry and thermogravimetric analysis measure the interaction of a material and heat.

量热法和热重分析测量材料和热之间的作用。

7. Separation 分离

Separation processes are used to decrease the complexity of material mixtures. Chromatography and electrophoresis are representative of this field.

分离处理用来减少混合材料中的复杂性。色谱和电泳是其中的代表。

8. Hybrid techniques 杂合技术

Combinations of the above techniques produce"hybrid"or"hyphenated"techniques.

组合以上技术产生杂合或者联用技术。

High-performance liquid chromatography/mass spectrometry (HPLC/MS)
高效液相色谱－质谱联用
Gas chromatography-mass spectrometry (GC-MS)
气相色谱－质谱联用
Chromatography-diode-array detection (LC-DAD)
色谱－二极管阵列检测联用
Capillary electrophoresis-mass spectrometry (CE-MS)
毛细管电泳－质谱联用
Capillary electrophoresis-ultraviolet-visible spectroscopy (CE-UV)
毛细管－紫外可见光谱联用

9. Lab-on-a-chip 芯片实验室

Devices that integrate multiple laboratory functions on a single chip of only a few square millimeters or centimeters in size and that are capable of handling extremely small fluid volumes down to less than picoliters.

芯片实验室是一种装置,在只有几个平方毫米或厘米尺寸的一个芯片上集成了多个实验室功能,能够操控小于皮升极少的液流。

与此相关的一些词汇有 biochip 生物芯片、microfludics chip 微流控芯片、MEMS(Micro-Electro-Mechanical System)微电机系统、NEMS(Nano-Electro-Mechanical System)纳电机系统。

10. 仪器常用术语

(1) Principal specifications of SEM 扫描电镜主要参数

Resolution 分辨率、magnification 放大倍数、accelerating Voltage 加速电压、probe Current 探针束流、maximum specimen size 最大样品尺寸、field of View 视场、ultimate pressure 真空度、specimen-exchange evacuation time 换样抽真空时间、accessories 可配附件

(2) Specifications of ESM 电化学扫描电镜参数

Maximum potential 最大电压、maximum current 最大电流、applied potential ranges 施加电压范围、applied potential resolution 施加电压分辨率、applied potential accuracy 施加电压准确度、applied potential noise 施加电压噪音、input impedance 输出阻抗、input bandwidth 输出带宽、scan rate 扫描范围、frequency 频率、amplitude 振幅

30　常用化学仪器装置

1. 常规仪器

有几个词常用来表示仪器或装置：instrument、device、equipment、appatus。

> equipment 和 equal，一个表示设备/器材，一个表示相等，它们之间有关联吗？
> equal 相等的/平等的/等于、equality 等量、equalization 均分、equilibrium 平衡、equivalent 相等的/当量
> equip 装备/配备。原意为装船、整齐摆放、使一致、使平衡、使相等。
> equipment 设备/器材。原意为整齐码放的东西。
> equiparation 均分/匀配
> equilibrium 平衡/均势/平静
> equipage 用具/化妆品，早期指在盒子里整齐排列有镊子、牙签、耳挖、指甲剪等物品的套装。
> 有几个单词与天平、秤或平衡有关：balance 平衡/天平、equal 相等的/等于、even 公平/偶数/相等、horizontal 水平的/同层的、lever 杠杆/秤、scale 天平/秤盘/刻度
> just 公平的/刚好、justice 法官/公正/公平、judge 审判/评价
> 对以上词汇的溯源分析，我们可以看出其中的关联：
> 天平是通过两端平衡来称重的，代表了相等、平衡；
> 天平也代表了正义、公平和司法，在古埃及、古希腊和古罗马神话中分别代表了正义女神玛特、忒弥斯和朱斯提提亚（Justitia）；
> 为了保证船的安全，装船时要称量货物并整齐码放，分别使得前后、左右等重，保持船体水平；
> 盒子里整齐码放的套装就像装船时货物的码放类似；
> 仪器、装置是由装在箱子里的各种配件组装而成的，天平几乎是化学史上最早使用的装置。

meter 常用来表示小型的便携式的仪器，一般翻译为"计"或"仪"。
sensor 传感器、biosensor 生物传感器

analytical balance 分析天平、bechtop 超净工作台、bio-reactor 生物反应器、centrifuge 离心机、chemiluminescence apparatus 化学发光仪、compact variable-speed microcentrifuges 台式小型离心机、constant temperature circulator 恒温循环泵、constant temperature water bath 恒温水浴锅、CO_2 Incubators CO_2 培养箱、electric furnace 电炉、electric sterilizer 高压灭菌锅、Fermenter 发酵罐、equal arm balance 托盘天平、freeze drying equipment 冻干机、high-speed programmable universal centrifuge 高速离心机、homogenizer 匀浆器、inverted microscope 倒置显微镜、low temperature programmable universal centrifuge 冷冻离心机、muffle furnace 马孚炉、platform balance 托盘天平、shaker 摇床、tuibidity 浊度计、stable temperature horizontal shaking bath 恒温水浴振荡器、stirrer 搅拌器、storage dewars 储藏用液氮罐、ultrahigh purity filter 超滤器、ultra-low temperature freezer 超低温冰箱、ultrasonic cleaner 超声波清洗器、vacuum drying oven 真空干燥箱、variable-speed shaker 混匀器、viscometer 黏度计

blowers 排风机、fume hoods 通风柜、laboratory furniture 实验台、storage cabinet 保管柜

2. 玻璃器皿或装置

adjustable-volume pipettor 可调移液器、alcohol burner 酒精灯、beaker 烧杯、Buchaer funnel 布氏漏斗、burette 滴定管、casserole 勺皿、cell culture flask 培养瓶、comparison tube 比色管、condenser 冷凝器、crucible 坩埚、desiccator 干燥器、developing tank 层析缸、disposable pipet with rubber squeezing bulb 胶帽滴管、drop-dispenser 滴管、dropping funnel 滴液漏斗、dryer 干燥剂、drying tube 干燥管、erlenmeyer 锥形瓶、evaporating dish 蒸发皿、glass rod/glass stick 玻棒、glass funnel 玻璃漏斗、grad cylinder 量筒、graduated pipette 刻度吸管、mortar 研钵、quartz sampling cell 石英比色皿、pestle 杵、culture dish 培养皿、pipette 移液管、pipette tips 枪头、wash bottle 洗瓶、reagent bottle 试剂瓶、round-buttom flask 圆颈烧瓶、rubber suction bulb 洗耳球、separatory funnel 分液漏斗、sprayer/atomizer 喷雾器、stopcock 活塞、stainless steel tray 不锈钢盘、test tube 试管、test tube clamp 试管夹、test tube rack 试管架、transfer pipet 移液管、volumetric flask 容量瓶、weighing bottle 称量瓶

> scale、grade 与割和格
>
> scale 也表示天平,还有秤盘、刻度、级别、比例、鱼鳞等含义,那么秤盘、刻度和鱼鳞之间有什么关系呢?原来 scale 是指天平的秤盘和横杆上的刻度,秤盘是薄片状的,和鱼鳞相似;刻度是一格一格的,鱼鳞也是一格一格的。
>
> scale 来自古印欧语词根(s)kel-,有 cut 割、刻画的意思。从字母的象形起源来说,字母 C 来自弯刀,有切割之意;字母 S 来自蛇,由蛇牙的锋利派生出切割之意。
>
> 字母 sc-常常组合在一起,表示与切、割相关的含义,如 scrape,表示擦、刮、擦去、擦伤、刮破。
>
> 由此可见单词 scale 和 cell 应有关联,因为无论是"鱼鳞"还是"细胞"均有一格一格的意思。
>
> 考虑到字母 C、G 的相互转化,很容易理解字母"g"开头的很多单词也具有刻度、一格一格、一步一步的含义,其在单词中的发音与汉字"刻""格"相似,比如:
>
> 比较 graduated cylinder 量筒和 graduated pipette 刻度吸量管这两个单词,注意到都有 graduated,我们都知道 graduate 是毕业或者研究生的意思,它和量筒、刻度吸管有什么关系呢?
>
> 原来 graduate 与 grade 同源,来自共同的古印欧语词根,原意为走,一步一步地走,从而衍生出分级,分步的含义,因此:
>
> grade 表示阶段、等级、排列、年级。
>
> graduate 表示量筒、渐变、毕业、研究生等含义,均有分步分阶段、一级一级变化的意思。

lab coat 实验大褂、lab marker/marking pen 实验室标记笔、mask 口罩、mortar 研钵、parafilm wrap 封口膜、pestle 杵、scissors 剪刀、syringe 注射器、tweezer 镊子、vinyl gloves 手套、weighing paper 称量纸、weighing spatula/spoon 称量勺

31 化 学 试 剂

chemicals 化学药品/化学品、reagent 试剂

1. 世界知名化学试剂商

(1) 美国 Sigma-Aldrich 公司是全球最大的化学试剂供应商，旗下包括 Sigma、Aldrich、Fluka、Rdh 等数个品牌，产品基本覆盖了化学试剂的各个领域。
(2) 欧洲 Acros
(3) 日本 TCI,东京化成工业株式会社
(4) 德国 Merck
(5) 英国 Alfa
(6) 美国 Fisher

2. 试剂纯度分级

AR（Analytical reagent 分析纯）、BC（Biochemical 生化试剂）、BP（British Pharmacopoeia 英国药典）、BR（Biological reagent 生物试剂）、BS（Biological Stain 生物染色剂）、CP（Chemical pure 化学纯）、EP（Extra Pure 特纯）、FCM（For Complexometry 络合滴定用）、FCP（For chromatography purpose 层析用）、FMP（For microscopic purpose 显微镜用）、FS（For synthesis 合成用）、GC（Gas chromatography 气相色谱）、GR（Guaranteed reagent 优级纯）、HPLC（High Preussuer Liquid chromatography 高压液相色谱）、Ind（Indicator 指示剂）、LR（Laboratory reagent 实验试剂）、OSA（Organic analyfical standard 有机分析标准）、PA（Pro analysis 分析用）、Pract（Practical use 实习用）、PT（Primary eragent 基准试剂）、Pur（Pure purum 纯）、Puriss（Purissmum 特纯）、SP（Spectrum pure 光谱纯）、Tech（Techincal grade 工业用）、TLC（Thin Layer chromatography 薄层色谱）、UV（Ultra violet pure 分光纯、光学纯、紫析分光光度纯）

Technical grade: These products are suitable for non-critical tasks in the laboratory such as rinsing, dissolving or are used as raw materials in production tasks.

工业级：在实验室中用于不太重要的任务，如清洗、溶解或者作为提纯的原

材料。

Synthesis reagents: Those reagents those are suitable for organic synthesis and preparative applications.

合成试剂：适用于有机合成与预备性应用的试剂。

Extra Pure grade: This quality is associated to products that are suitable for qualitative and semi-quantitative grades. These chemicals suitable for general laboratory works, and in most cases, meet Most Pharmacopoeia (BP, USP etc.) Standards.

超纯级：适用于定性和半定量级别的产品。用于一般性实验室任务，满足大多数药典标准。

Pharmacopoeia Grade: Products and solutions meeting the purity requirements of chemical products admitted in the pharmaceutical sector (pharmacopoeia requirement such as NF, BP, USP, Ph Eur, DAB, DAC, JP, Ph Franc..)

药典级：满足医药行业药典纯度要求的化学品。

ACS reagent: Reagents meets the specification of American Chemical Society (ACS).

ACS试剂：满足美国化学会要求的试剂。

HPLC reagent: Product range is specially made for high performance liquid chromatography.

高效液相色谱试剂：专门用于高效液相色谱的一类产品。

Spectroscopy grade: Solvents display a high UV permeability and are subject to strict IR Spectroscopy tests.

光谱级：经过严格红外光谱测试具有高紫外透过率的溶剂。

3. 水

配制化学试剂常常要用到不同级别的水：

(1) Primary grade water 初级水

Primary grade water has the lowest level of purity, and normally has a conductivity of $1 \sim 50$ μS/cm. It can be produced by single weakly basic anion exchange resins or by reverse osmosis.

初级水纯度最低，通常导电率为 $1 \sim 50$ μS/cm。它可以用弱碱性阴离子交换树脂或反向渗透法制备。

(2) Deionized water 去离子水

Deionized water typically has a conductivity of 1.0 to 0.1 μS/cm (i.e. a resistivity of 1.0 to 10.0 MΩcm), and is produced by mixed-bed ion exchange using strongly basic anion exchange resins.

去离子水的导电率通常在 1.0 和 0.1 μS/cm 之间。采用强碱性阴离子交换树脂经过混合床离子交换制得。

(3) General laboratory grade water 一般实验室级水

General laboratory grade water not only has high purity in ionic terms, but low levels of organic compounds and micro-organisms. A typical specification would be a conductivity of < 1.0 μS/cm (resistivity > 1.0 MΩ-cm), a total organic carbon (TOC) content of less than 50 ppb and a bacterial count below 1 CFU/ml.

一般实验室级水不仅仅在离子方面高纯度,在有机物和微生物方面含量也低。典型的导电率规格小于 1.0 μS/cm,总有机碳含量少于 50 ppb,细菌计数低于 1 CFU/ml。

(4) Ultra-pure grade water 超纯水

The Ultra pure water is deionised and demineralised water. It was produced using a reverse osmosis, ion exchange and organic scavenging to ensure the highest level of purity. Ultra-pure grade water is required for a variety of sensitive analytical techniques such as high performance liquid chromatography (HPLC), ion chromatography (IC) and inductively coupled mass spectrometry (ICP-MS).

超纯水是去离子去矿物质的水。采用反向渗透、离子交换和有机物净化获得高纯度。主要用于灵敏的分析仪器如 HPLC,IC 和 ICP-MS。

32 化 学 论 文

1. 作品种类

bible/canon 圣经/权威著作,其中 Bible 常特指基督教经典《圣经》,Canon 也被全球领先的生产影像与信息产品的佳能集团所使用。

works 著作、book 书、thesis/dissertation 毕业论文、paper 论文、conference abstract 会议摘要、proceedings 会议论文集、memorandum 备忘录

manuscript 手稿、monograph 专题文章

2. 投稿相关词汇

为了方便和指导作者投稿,一般期刊都会提供一个作者须知,称之为 author guidelines/notice to authors/information for authors/guide for authors,主要内容如下:

(1) scope

aims and scope 目的和范围,主要介绍期刊的定位和覆盖内容,有时也用 description 简介。

audience 目标读者、impact factor 影响因子、abstract and indexing 摘录和索引

editoral board 编委会、editorial advisory board member/editorial board member/member of editorial board 编委、editorial advisor 编辑顾问

editor 编辑、chief editor/editor in chief 主编、associate editor-in-chief/associate editor/managing editor 副主编

(2) 道德规范与政策

ethics in publishing 出版道德规范、policy and ethics 政策与道德规范、editorial policy 编辑政策

plagiarism 剽窃,说明对剽窃的态度和定义。

conflict of interest 利益冲突,要求作者就可能的利益冲突做出说明。

submission declaration 投稿声明,表明稿件没有同时投到其他刊物或者已经出版。

changes to authorship 作者变更,变更作者需给出合适的理由。

copyright 版权,就版权归属做出说明。

Journal Publishing Agreement 期刊出版协议,文章出版前作者需要签署该协议。

referee 审稿人,作者需要提供几个可能的审稿人。

comment/review 审稿

(3) types of papers 文章类型

Full papers should describe original research work not previously published, and should be complete descriptions of full investigations comprising around 5 000 words and with up to 6 figures and/or tables.

全长文章应该介绍起先没有出版过的原创性工作,对一个全面的研究进行充分地描述,大约 5 000 字,最多 6 个图或表。

Short Communications should be concise but complete descriptions of original limited investigations comprising around 3 000 words with up to 3 figures and/or tables.

短的通讯应该对一个原创性的有限调查进行精炼而全面地描述,大约 3 000 字,最多 3 个图或表。

Review Articles should comprehensively cover a subjcct of current interest, comprise around 8 000 words and be extensively referenced. Contributions may be submitted or invited.

综述文章应该全面覆盖一个当前兴趣的主题,大约 8 000 字,充分地文献引用。可以直接投稿也可以约稿。

(4) 文章结构

title 题目

author names and affliations 作者姓名和单位、corresponding author 通讯作者

abstract 摘要、Key terms/keyword 关键词

contents/table of contents/catalogue/catalog/list 目录

introduction 前言、material and methods 材料和方法、results 结果、discussion 讨论、conclusions 结论、Acknowledgements 致谢

---

conclusion 由 con-和-clusion 组成,前者表示共同的,后者来自 clude 表示关闭。-clude 与 cover 覆盖、close 关闭等词汇同源,均有"以手覆盖"的意思,派生词汇包括:

include 包括、exclude 排除、conclude 总结、occlude 堵塞、preclude 阻止

---

reference/literature 参考文献、appendix 附录阑尾、bibliography 书目

nomenclature and units 术语和单位、math formulae 数学公式、footnotes 脚注、artwork 插图、figure captions 插图图题、table 表、schematic diagram 示意图

（5）投稿与接受

submit 投稿、proof 校样稿、in press/in publication 出版中、offprint 单行本、

received 收到、accepted 接受：这两个词有区别，前者只表示收到而已，后者才表示同意接受准备出版。

Digital Object Identifier (DOI) 意为"数字对象标识符"，用来标志在数字环境中的内容对象，文章一旦接受就会有一个 DOI 地址。

3. 著名出版社和期刊

（1）American Chemical Society/ACS(http://pubs.acs.org/)

美国化学会拥有世界顶级的化学类期刊，如著名的 Journal of the American Chemical Society(JACS)美国化学会志，顶级的综述性刊物 Chemical Reviews 化学评论等。旗下代表性期刊如下：

Accounts of Chemical Research

ACS Applied Materials & Interfaces

ACS Catalysis

ACS Chemical Biology

ACS Chemical Neuroscience

ACS Combinatorial Science

ACS Macro Letters

ACS Medicinal Chemistry Letters

ACS Nano

Advances in Chemistry

Analytical Chemistry

Biochemistry

Bioconjugate Chemistry

Biomacromolecules

Biotechnology Progress

Chemical Research in Toxicology

Chemical Reviews

Chemistry of Materials

Crystal Growth & Design

Energy & Fuels

Environmental Science & Technology

Industrial & Engineering Chemistry

Inorganic Chemistry

Journal of the American Chemical Society

Journal of Agricultural and Food Chemistry

Journal of Chemical Education

Journal of Medicinal Chemistry

Journal of Natural Products

The Journal of Organic Chemistry

The Journal of Physical Chemistry A

The Journal of Physical Chemistry B

The Journal of Physical Chemistry C

Journal of Proteome Research

Langmuir

Macromolecules

Nano Letters

Organic Letters

Organometallics

（2）Wiley-VCH 出版公司（http://www.wiley-vch.de）

该出版公司拥有许多世界著名刊物，特别是 German Chemical Society (GDCh)德国化学会的 Angewandte Chemie 德国化学会志。旗下代表性期刊如下：

Advanced Functional Materials

Advanced Materials

Advanced Materials Interfaces

Advanced Synthesis & Catalysis

Angewandte Chemie

Angewandte Chemie International Edition

Biotechnology Journal

Chemical Engineering & Technology

Chemistry-A European Journal

Chemistry-An Asian Journal

Electroanalysis

ELECTROPHORESIS
European Journal of Organic Chemistry
Fuel Cells
Journal of Separation Science
Macromolecular Bioscience
Macromolecular Chemistry and Physics
Macromolecular Materials and Engineering
Macromolecular Rapid Communications
Materials and Corrosion
PROTEOMICS
Single Molecules
Small

(3) Royal Society of Chemistry 英国皇家化学会(http://www.rsc.org/)
Analyst
Biomaterials Science
Chemical Communications
Chemical Society Reviews
CrystEngComm
Dalton Transactions
Journal of Materials Chemistry
Journal of Materials Chemistry A
Journal of Materials Chemistry B
Journal of Materials Chemistry C
Journal of the Chemical Society
Lab on a Chip
Metallomics
Nanoscale
Physical Chemistry Chemical Physics
Polymer Chemistry
RSC Advances
Soft Matter
Toxicology Research
Transactions of the Faraday Society

33 化学会议

1. 会议种类

表达会议的英文相关的词汇很多,但它们之间有一些微妙的区别:

(1) conference 会议

A conference is a meeting, often lasting a few days, which is organized on a particular subject or to bring together people who have a common interest.

conference 表示会议,通常持续几天,有一个特定的主题,将有共同爱好目的的人聚集到一起。

一般规模较大,比较正式。

(2) symposium 专题讨论会

A symposium is a conference in which experts or academics discuss a particular subject.

symposium 会议上专家或学者就一特定主题进行讨论。

与 conference 相比较,symposium 一般更狭义特指某一范围,在规模上专题会比 conference 小。

(3) seminar 研讨会/讲座

规模较小,类似课堂的学术会议,一般是发言者演讲,同时其他的人先听之后参与讨论或发问。

(4) lecture 演讲/讲座

A lecture is a talk someone gives in order to teach people about a particular subject.

lecture 是一个演讲或讲座,目的是将特定内容传授给听众。

仅由一位专家来作报告,报告后不一定会接受观众的提问。

(5) workshop 研习会

由几个人进行密集讨论的集会,通常需当场做练习,如:国际礼仪、站姿等等。

(6) meeting 会议

A meeting is an event in which a group of people come together to discuss things or make decisions.

meeting 是一群人聚到一起讨论事情并做决定。

(7) congress 国会/议会/代表大会

由专属国家的,政府或非政府组织的代表或委员参加。它的举办是为了讨论争端,计划和公众利益。通常规模大,有代表性,范围广。

(8) convention 会议

A convention is a large meeting of an organization or political group.

convention 是组织或政治团体的大型会议。

(9) forum 论坛/讨论会

A forum is a situation in which people exchange ideas and discuss issues, especially important public issues.

论坛实际上是一种公众集会,在那里人们交换思想,讨论问题,特别是重要的公众问题。

2. 会议组织

以一个国际会议为例。会议主要内容结构如下:

(1)会议基本信息

主要是名称、时间、地点和网址,如图 33.1 所示。

图 33.1

(2) 邀请信

主要目的是发出邀请、告知内容、参会须知、联系方式等。

Developing Learning Communities in the Chemical Sciences

We cordially invite you to participate in the 23rd IUPAC International Conference on Chemistry Education to be held at the Metro Toronto Convention Centre from 13-18 July, 2014. This will be the first time since 1989 that this conference has come to Canada.

The theme of the conference is communications. Our goal is to investigate how best to forge global links in the chemistry teaching and learning communities and to consider best practices in exploiting technological advances in communications in order to establish innovative learning partnerships. Symposia will focus on communication amongst chemistry professionals, educators, students and the lay community.

Symposia and workshops that support these themes are solicited. Your ideas are key to making ICCE 2014 a productive and successful event. We look forward to hearing your thoughts on the development of the conference program.

The conference will consist of plenary lectures, submitted oral and poster presentations, panel discussions, roundtable discussions as well as an exhibition. Recently renovated, state-of-the art laboratories at the University of Toronto are available for practical workshops.

We look forward to welcoming the global chemical education community to Canada.

Andrew Dicks, Co-Chair
Judith Poë, Co-Chair

Contact Information
Andy Dicks
Co-chair of the organizing committee
Department of Chemistry
University of Toronto
80 St. George Street
Toronto, ON
M5S 3H6
Canada
E-mail: icce2014@chem.utoronto.ca

(3) 会议主题

Six general conference themes

Communicating across the Educational Levels
Outreach to the Lay Community
International Student Learning Communities
Technological Support of Chemistry Learning and Learning Communities
Greening Attitudes in Chemistry Education
Interdisciplinary Collaborations

---

(4) 重要的日期
提醒拟参会者注意关键日期。

Important Dates

Jan. 31 2014
registration opens
Feb. 21 2014
deadline for abstract submission
Mar. 2014
notice of abstract acceptance
May 15 2014
deadline for early registration fees
May 2014
workshop registration opens
July 13-18 2014
ICCE 2014

---

(5) 注册须知
注册登记、注册费说明等信息。

Registration Fees

Registration is now open. Registration fees include over five days of scientific programming with admission to poster sessions/exhibitions, the conference book, a welcome reception at the University of Toronto on Sunday July 13, and lunch/coffee breaks on July 14-18. The two-day high school teacher registration includes admission to scientific sessions/exhibitions for two days, the conference book, and lunch/coffee breaks for two days.

Click here to register or Downloadable registration form

Wednesday July 16: Empress of Canada Boat Cruise

	Early Bird (Jan. 31-May 15)	Standard (May 16-Jul. 12)	On-site (Jul. 13-18)
Regular registration	$550	$600	$700
IUPAC member	$495	$540	$630
Participants from developing countries	$320	$350	$400
Retired person	$320	$350	$400
High school teacher-full conference	$320	$350	$400
High school teacher-two days only	$160	$175	$200
Student	$320	$350	$400
Accompanying persons	$50	$75	$100

Wednesday July 16: Empress of Canada Boat Cruise

(6) 其他信息

accommodation 住宿、venue/travel 旅行、committee 组委会、sponsors 赞助商、program 会议程序、exhibitors 展厅、abstract submission 摘要投稿

34 无机化学*

Inorganic chemistry

From Wikipedia[①], the free encyclopedia

Inorganic chemistry is the study of the synthesis and behavior of inorganic and organometallic compounds. This field covers all chemical compounds except the myriad organic compounds (carbon based compounds, usually containing C-H bonds), which are the subjects of organic chemistry. The distinction between the two disciplines is far from absolute, and there is much overlap, most importantly in the sub-discipline of organometallic chemistry. It has applications in every aspect of the chemical industry-including catalysis, materials science, pigments, surfactants, coatings, medicine, fuel, and agriculture.

Contents

1 Key concepts
    1.1 Industrial inorganic chemistry
2 Descriptive inorganic chemistry
    2.1 Coordination compounds
    2.2 Main group compounds
    2.3 Transition metal compounds
    2.4 Organometallic compounds
    2.5 Cluster compounds
    2.6 Bioinorganic compounds
    2.7 Solid state compounds
3 Theoretical inorganic chemistry

---

① 虽然维基百科的内容可以自由编辑,严谨性有待推敲,但仍有值得借鉴之处。许多科学词汇的条目信息较为系统,具有很高的参考价值。本书有意选取几个词条作为范文,供自由阅读所需,在学习过程中注意批判性学习。

3.1 Qualitative theories
3.2 Molecular symmetry group theory
4 Thermodynamics and inorganic chemistry
5 Mechanistic inorganic chemistry
　　5.1 Main group elements and lanthanides
　　5.2 Transition metal complexes
　　　　5.2.1 Redox reactions
　　　　5.2.2 Reactions at ligands
6 Characterization of inorganic compounds
7 Synthetic inorganic chemistry
8 See also
9 References

Key concepts

Many inorganic compounds are ionic compounds, consisting of cations and anions joined by ionic bonding. Examples of salts (which are ionic compounds) are magnesium chloride $MgCl_2$, which consists of magnesium cations Mg^{2+} and chloride anions Cl^-; or sodium oxide Na_2O, which consists of sodium cations Na^+ and oxide anions O^{2-}. In any salt, the proportions of the ions are such that the electric charges cancel out, so that the bulk compound is electrically neutral. The ions are described by their oxidation state and their ease of formation can be inferred from the ionization potential (for cations) or from the electron affinity (anions) of the parent elements.

Important classes of inorganic salts are the oxides, the carbonates, the sulfates and the halides. Many inorganic compounds are characterized by high melting points. Inorganic salts typically are poor conductors in the solid state. Other important features include their solubility in water(see: solubility chart) and ease of crystallization. Where some salts (e.g., NaCl) are very soluble in water, others (e.g., SiO_2) are not.

The simplest inorganic reaction is double displacement when in mixing of two salts the ions are swapped without a change in oxidation state. In redox reactions one reactant, the oxidant, lowers its oxidation state and another reactant, the reductant, has its oxidation state increased. The net result is an exchange of electrons. Electron exchange can occur indirectly as well, e. g. , in batteries, a key concept in electrochemistry.

When one reactant contains hydrogen atoms, a reaction can take place by exchanging protons in acid-base chemistry. In a more general definition, an acid can be any chemical species capable of binding to electron pairs is called a Lewis acid; conversely any molecule that tends to donate an electron pair is referred to as a Lewis base. As a refinement of acid-base interactions, the HSAB theory takes into account polarizability and size of ions.

Inorganic compounds are found in nature as minerals. Soil may contain iron sulfide as pyrite or calcium sulfate as gypsum. Inorganic compounds are also found multitasking as biomolecules: as electrolytes (sodium chloride), in energy storage (ATP) or in construction (the polyphosphate backbone in DNA).

The first important man-made inorganic compound was ammonium nitrate for soil fertilization through the Haber process. Inorganic compounds are synthesized for use as catalysts such as vanadium(V) oxide and titanium(III) chloride, or as reagents in organic chemistry such as lithium aluminium hydride.

<u>Subdivisions of inorganic chemistry are organometallic chemistry, cluster chemistry and bioinorganic chemistry.</u> These fields are active areas of research in inorganic chemistry, aimed toward new catalysts, superconductors, and therapies.

Industrial inorganic chemistry

Inorganic chemistry is a highly practical area of science. Traditionally, the scale of a nation's economy could be evaluated by their productivity of sulfuric acid. The top 20 inorganic chemicals manufactured in Canada, China, Europe, India, Japan, and the US (2005 data): aluminium sulfate, ammonia, ammonium nitrate, ammonium sulfate, carbon black, chlorine, hydrochloric acid, hydrogen, hydrogen peroxide, nitric acid, nitrogen, oxygen, phosphoric acid, sodium carbonate, sodium chlorate, sodium hydroxide, sodium silicate, sodium sulfate, sulfuric acid, and titanium dioxide.

The manufacturing of fertilizers is another practical application of industrial inorganic chemistry.

Descriptive inorganic chemistry

Descriptive inorganic chemistry focuses on the classification of compounds based on their properties. Partly the classification focuses on the position in the periodic table of the heaviest element (the element with the highest atomic weight) in the compound, partly by grouping compounds by their structural similarities. When studying inorganic compounds, one often encounters parts of the different classes of inorganic chemistry (an organometallic compound is characterized by its coordination chemistry, and may show interesting solid state properties).

Different classifications are:

Coordination compounds

Classical coordination compounds feature metals bound to "lone pairs" of electrons residing on the main group atoms of ligands such as H_2O, NH_3, Cl^-, and CN^-. In modern coordination compounds almost all organic and inorganic compounds can be used as ligands. The "metal" usually is a metal from the groups 3-13, as well as the trans-lanthanides and trans-actinides, but from a certain perspective, all chemical compounds can be described as coordination complexes.

The stereochemistry of coordination complexes can be quite rich, as hinted at by Werner's separation of two enantiomers of $[Co((OH)_2Co(NH_3)_4)_3]^{6+}$, an early demonstration that chirality is not inherent to organic compounds. A topical theme within this specialization is supramolecular coordination chemistry.

Examples: $[Co(EDTA)]^-$, $[Co(NH_3)_6]^{3+}$, $TiCl_4(THF)_2$.

Main group compounds

These species feature elements from groups 1, 2 and 13-18 (excluding hydrogen) of the periodic table. Due to their often similar reactivity, the elements in group 3 (Sc, Y, and La) and group 12 (Zn, Cd, and Hg) are also generally included.

Main group compounds have been known since the beginnings of chemistry, e. g. , elemental sulfur and the distillable white phosphorus. Experiments on oxygen, O_2, by Lavoisier and Priestley not only identified an important diatomic gas, but opened the way for describing compounds and reactions according to stoichiometric ratios. The discovery of a practical synthesis of ammonia using iron catalysts by Carl Bosch and Fritz Haber in the early 1 900 s deeply impacted mankind, demonstrating the significance of inorganic chemical synthesis. Typical main group compounds are SiO_2, $SnCl_4$, and N_2O. Many main group compounds can also be classed as "organometallic", as they contain organic groups, e. g., $B(CH_3)_3$. Main group compounds also occur in nature, e. g., phosphate in DNA, and therefore may be classed as bioinorganic. Conversely, organic compounds lacking (many) hydrogen ligands can be classed as "inorganic", such as the fullerenes, buckytubes and binary carbon oxides.

Examples: tetrasulfur tetranitride S_4N_4, diborane B_2H_6, silicones, buckminsterfullerene C_{60}.

Transition metal compounds

Compounds containing metals from group 4 to 11 are considered transition metal compounds. Compounds with a metal from group 3 or 12 are sometimes also incorporated into this group, but also often classified as main group compounds.

Transition metal compounds show a rich coordination chemistry, varying from tetrahedral for titanium (e. g., $TiCl_4$) to square planar for some nickel complexes to octahedral for coordination complexes of cobalt. A range of transition metals can be found in biologically important compounds, such as iron in hemoglobin.

Examples: iron pentacarbonyl, titanium tetrachloride, cisplatin

Organometallic compounds

Usually, organometallic compounds are considered to contain the M-C-H group. The metal (M) in these species can either be a main group element or a transition metal. Operationally, the definition of an organometallic compound is more relaxed to include also highly lipophilic complexes such as metal carbonyls and even metal alkoxides.

Organometallic compounds are mainly considered a special category because organic ligands are often sensitive to hydrolysis or oxidation, necessitating that organometallic chemistry employs more specialized preparative methods than was traditional in Werner-type complexes. Synthetic methodology, especially the ability to manipulate complexes in solvents of low coordinating power, enabled the exploration of very weakly coordinating ligands such as hydrocarbons, H_2, and N_2. Because the ligands are petrochemicals in some sense, the area of organometallic chemistry has greatly benefited from its relevance to industry.

Examples: Cyclopentadienyliron dicarbonyl dimer $(C_5H_5)Fe(CO)_2CH_3$, Ferrocene $Fe(C_5H_5)_2$, Molybdenum hexacarbonyl $Mo(CO)_6$, Diborane B_2H_6, Tetrakis(triphenylphosphine)palladium(0) $Pd[P(C_6H_5)_3]_4$

Cluster compounds

Clusters can be found in all classes of chemical compounds. According to the commonly accepted definition, a cluster consists minimally of a triangular set of atoms that are directly bonded to each other. But metal-metal bonded dimetallic complexes are highly relevant to the area. Clusters occur in "pure" inorganic systems, organometallic chemistry, main group chemistry, and bioinorganic chemistry. The distinction between very large clusters and bulk solids is increasingly blurred. This interface is the chemical basis of nanoscience or nanotechnology and specifically arise from the study of quantum size effects in cadmium selenide clusters. Thus, large clusters can be described as an array of bound atoms intermediate in character between a molecule and a solid.

Examples: $Fe_3(CO)_{12}$, $B_{10}H_{14}$, $[Mo_6Cl_{14}]^{2-}$, 4Fe-4S

Bioinorganic compounds

By definition, these compounds occur in nature, but the subfield includes anthropogenic species, such as pollutants (e. g. , methylmercury) and drugs (e. g. , Cisplatin). The field, which incorporates many aspects of biochemistry, includes many kinds of compounds, e. g. , the phosphates in DNA, and also metal complexes containing ligands that range from biological macromolecules, commonly peptides, to ill-defined species such as humic acid, and to water (e. g. , coordinated to gadolinium complexes employed for MRI). Traditionally bioinorganic chemistry focuses on electron-and energy-transfer in proteins relevant to respiration. Medicinal inorganic chemistry includes the study of both non-essential and essential elements with applications to diagnosis and therapies.

Examples: hemoglobin, methylmercury, carboxypeptidase

Solid state compounds

$YBa_2Cu_3O_7$, or YBCO, is a high temperature superconductor able to levitate above a magnet when colder than its critical temperature of about 90 K (-183 °C).

This important area focuses on structure, bonding, and the physical properties of materials. In practice, solid state inorganic chemistry uses techniques such as crystallography to gain an understanding of the properties that result from collective interactions between the subunits of the solid. Included in solid state chemistry are metals and their alloys or intermetallic derivatives. Related fields are condensed matter physics, mineralogy, and materials science.

Examples: silicon chips, zeolites, $YBa_2Cu_3O_7$

Characterization of inorganic compounds

Because of the diverse range of elements and the correspondingly diverse properties of the resulting derivatives, inorganic chemistry is closely associated with many methods of analysis. Older methods tended to examine bulk properties such as the electrical conductivity of solutions, melting points, solubility, and acidity. With the advent of quantum theory and the corresponding expansion of electronic apparatus, new tools have been introduced to probe the electronic properties of inorganic molecules and solids. Often these measurements provide insights relevant to theoretical models. For example, measurements on the photoelectron spectrum of methane demonstrated that describing the bonding by the two-center, two-electron bonds predicted between the carbon and hydrogen using Valence Bond Theory is not appropriate for describing ionisation processes in a simple way. Such insights led to the popularization of molecular orbital theory as fully delocalised orbitals are a more appropriate simple description of electron removal and electron excitation.

Commonly encountered techniques are:

X-ray crystallography: This technique allows for the 3D determination of molecular structures.

Dual polarisation interferometer: This technique measures the conformation and conformational change of molecules.

Various forms of spectroscopy

Ultraviolet-visible spectroscopy: Historically, this has been an important tool, since many inorganic compounds are strongly colored

NMR spectroscopy: Besides ^1H and ^{13}C many other "good" NMR nuclei (e. g., ^{11}B, ^{19}F, ^{31}P, and ^{195}Pt) give important information on compound properties and structure. Also the NMR of paramagnetic species can result in important structural information. Proton NMR is also important because the light hydrogen nucleus is not easily detected by X-ray crystallography.

Infrared spectroscopy: Mostly for absorptions from carbonyl ligands

Electron nuclear double resonance (ENDOR) spectroscopy

Mössbauer spectroscopy

Electron-spin resonance: ESR (or EPR) allows for the measurement of the environment of paramagnetic metal centres.

Electrochemistry: Cyclic voltammetry and related techniques probe the redox characteristics of compounds.

Synthetic inorganic chemistry

Although some inorganic species can be obtained in pure form from nature, most are synthesized in chemical plants and in the laboratory.

Inorganic synthetic methods can be classified roughly according the volatility or solubility of the component reactants. Soluble inorganic compounds are prepared using methods of organic synthesis. For metal−containing compounds that are reactive toward air, Schlenk line and glove box techniques are followed. Volatile compounds and gases are manipulated in "vacuum manifolds" consisting of glass piping interconnected through valves, the entirety of which can be evacuated to 0.001 mm Hg or less. Compounds are condensed using liquid nitrogen (b. p. 78K) or other cryogens. Solids are typically prepared using tube furnaces, the reactants and products being sealed in containers, often made of fused silica (amorphous SiO_2) but sometimes more specialized materials such as welded Ta tubes or Pt "boats". Products and reactants are transported between temperature zones to drive reactions.

35 分析化学*

Analytical chemistry

From Wikipedia, the free encyclopedia

Analytical chemistry is the study of the separation, identification, and quantification of the chemical components of natural and artificial materials. Qualitative analysis gives an indication of the identity of the chemical species in the sample, and quantitative analysis determines the amount of certain components in the substance. The separation of components is often performed prior to analysis.

Analytical methods can be separated into classical and instrumental. Classical methods (also known as wet chemistry methods) use separations such as precipitation, extraction, and distillation and qualitative analysis by color, odor, or melting point. Classical quantitative analysis is achieved by measurement of weight or volume. Instrumental methods use an apparatus to measure physical quantities of the analyte such as light absorption, fluorescence, or conductivity. The separation of materials is accomplished using chromatography, electrophoresis or Field Flow Fractionation methods.

Analytical chemistry is also focused on improvements in experimental design, chemometrics, and the creation of new measurement tools to provide better chemical information. Analytical chemistry has applications in forensics, bioanalysis, clinical analysis, environmental analysis, and materials analysis.

Contents

1 History
2 Classical methods
   2.1 Qualitative analysis
      2.1.1 Chemical tests
      2.1.2 Flame test
   2.2 Quantitative analysis

2.2.1 Gravimetric analysis
2.2.2 Volumetric analysis
3 Instrumental methods
  3.1 Spectroscopy
  3.2 Mass spectrometry
  3.3 Electrochemical analysis
  3.4 Thermal analysis
  3.5 Separation
  3.6 Hybrid techniques
  3.7 Microscopy
  3.8 Lab-on-a-chip
4 Standards
  4.1 Standard curve
  4.2 Internal standards
  4.3 Standard addition
5 Signals and noise
  5.1 Thermal noise
  5.2 Shot noise
  5.3 Flicker noise
  5.4 Environmental noise
  5.5 Noise reduction
6 Applications
7 See also
8 References
9 Further reading
10 External links

History

Analytical chemistry has been important since the early days of chemistry, providing methods for determining which elements and chemicals are present in the object in question. During this period significant analytical contributions to chemistry include the development of systematic elemental analysis by Justus von Liebig and systematized organic analysis based on the specific reactions of functional groups.

The first instrumental analysis was flame emissive spectrometry developed by Robert Bunsen and Gustav Kirchhoff who discovered rubidium (Rb) and caesium (Cs) in 1860.

Most of the major developments in analytical chemistry take place after 1900. During this period instrumental analysis becomes progressively dominant in the field. In particular many of the basic spectroscopic and spectrometric techniques were discovered in the early 20th century and refined in the late 20th century.

The separation sciences follow a similar time line of development and also become increasingly transformed into high performance instruments. In the 1970s many of these techniques began to be used together to achieve a complete characterization of samples.

Starting in approximately the 1970s into the present day analytical chemistry has progressively become more inclusive of biological questions (bioanalytical chemistry), whereas it had previously been largely focused on inorganic or small organic molecules. Lasers have been increasingly used in chemistry as probes and even to start and influence a wide variety of reactions. The late 20th century also saw an expansion of the application of analytical chemistry from somewhat academic chemical questions to forensic, environmental, industrial and medical questions, such as in histology.

Modern analytical chemistry is dominated by instrumental analysis. Many analytical chemists focus on a single type of instrument. Academics tend to either focus on new applications and discoveries or on new methods of analysis. The discovery of a chemical present in blood that increases the risk of cancer would be a discovery that an analytical chemist might be involved in. An effort to develop a new method might involve the use of a tunable laser to increase the specificity and sensitivity of a spectrometric method. Many methods, once developed, are kept purposely static so that data can be compared over long periods of time. This is particularly true in industrial quality assurance (QA), forensic and environmental applications. Analytical chemistry plays an increasingly important role in the pharmaceutical industry where, aside from QA, it is used in discovery of new drug candidates and in clinical applications where understanding the interactions between the drug and the patient are critical.

Classical methods

Although modern analytical chemistry is dominated by sophisticated instrumentation, the roots of analytical chemistry and some of the principles used in modern instruments are from traditional techniques many of which are still used today. These techniques also tend to form the backbone of most undergraduate analytical chemistry educational labs.

Qualitative analysis

A qualitative analysis determines the presence or absence of a particular compound, but not the mass or concentration. By definition, qualitative analyses do not measure quantity.

Chemical tests

There are numerous qualitative chemical tests, for example, the acid test for gold and the Kastle-Meyer test for the presence of blood.

Flame test

Inorganic qualitative analysis generally refers to a systematic scheme to confirm the presence of certain, usually aqueous, ions or elements by performing a series of reactions that eliminate ranges of possibilities and then confirms suspected ions with a confirming test. Sometimes small carbon containing ions are included in such schemes. With modern instrumentation these tests are rarely used but can be useful for educational purposes and in field work or other situations where access to state-of-the-art instruments are not available or expedient.

Quantitative analysis

Gravimetric analysis

Gravimetric analysis involves determining the amount of material present by weighing the sample before and/or after some transformation. A common example used in undergraduate education is the determination of the amount of water in a hydrate by heating the sample to remove the water such that the difference in weight is due to the loss of water.

Volumetric analysis

Titration involves the addition of a reactant to a solution being analyzed until some equivalence point is reached. Often the amount of material in the solution being analyzed may be determined. Most familiar to those who have taken chemistry during secondary education is the acid-base titration involving a color changing indicator. There are many other types of titrations, for example potentiometric titrations. These titrations may use different types of indicators to reach some equivalence point.

Instrumental methods

Spectroscopy

Spectroscopy measures the interaction of the molecules with electromagnetic radiation. Spectroscopy consists of many different applications such as atomic absorption spectroscopy, atomic emission spectroscopy, ultraviolet-visible spectroscopy, x-ray fluorescence spectroscopy, infrared spectroscopy, Raman spectroscopy, dual polarisation interferometry, nuclear magnetic resonance spectroscopy, photoemission spectroscopy, Mössbauer spectroscopy and so on.

Mass spectrometry

Mass spectrometry measures mass-to-charge ratio of molecules using electric and magnetic fields. There are several ionization methods: electron impact, chemical ionization, electrospray, fast atom bombardment, matrix assisted laser desorption ionization, and others. Also, mass spectrometry is categorized by approaches of mass analyzers: magnetic-sector, quadrupole mass analyzer, quadrupole ion trap, time-of-flight, Fourier transform ion cyclotron resonance, and so on.

Electrochemical analysis

Electroanalytical methods measure the potential (volts) and/or current (amps) in an electrochemical cell containing the analyte. These methods can be categorized according to which aspects of the cell are controlled and which are measured. The three main categories are potentiometry (the difference in electrode potentials is measured), coulometry (the cell's current is measured over time), and voltammetry (the cell's current is measured while actively altering the cell's potential).

Thermal analysis

Calorimetry and thermogravimetric analysis measure the interaction of a material and heat.

Separation

Separation processes are used to decrease the complexity of material mixtures. Chromatography, electrophoresis and Field Flow Fractionation are representative of this field.

Hybrid techniques

Combinations of the above techniques produce a "hybrid" or "hyphenated" technique. Several examples are in popular use today and new hybrid techniques are under development. For example, gas chromatography-mass spectrometry, gas chromatography-infrared spectroscopy, liquid chromatography-mass spectrometry, liquid chromatography-NMR spectroscopy. liquid chromagraphy-infrared spectroscopy and capillary electrophoresis-mass spectrometry.

Hyphenated separation techniques refers to a combination of two (or more) techniques to detect and separate chemicals from solutions. Most often the other technique is some form of chromatography. Hyphenated techniques are widely used in chemistry and biochemistry. A slash is sometimes used instead of hyphen, especially if the name of one of the methods contains a hyphen itself.

Microscopy

The visualization of single molecules, single cells, biological tissues and nanomaterials is an important and attractive approach in analytical science. Also, hybridization with other traditional analytical tools is revolutionizing analytical science. Microscopy can be categorized into three different fields: optical microscopy, electron microscopy, and scanning probe microscopy. Recently, this field is rapidly progressing because of the rapid development of the computer and camera industries.

Lab-on-a-chip

Devices that integrate (multiple) laboratory functions on a single chip of only millimeters to a few square centimeters in size and that are capable of handling extremely small fluid volumes down to less than picoliters.

Standards

A general method for analysis of concentration involves the creation of a calibration curve. This allows for determination of the amount of a chemical in a material by comparing the results of unknown sample to those of a series of known standards. If the concentration of element or compound in a sample is too high for the detection range of the technique, it can simply be diluted in a pure solvent. If the amount in the sample is below an instrument's range of measurement, the method of addition can be used. In this method a known quantity of the element or compound under study is added, and the difference between the concentration added, and the concentration observed is the amount actually in the sample.

Internal standards

Sometimes an internal standard is added at a known concentration directly to an analytical sample to aid in quantitation. The amount of analyte present is then determined relative to the internal standard as a calibrant. An ideal internal standard is isotopically-enriched analyte which gives rise to the method of isotope dilution.

Standard addition

The method of standard addition is used in instrumental analysis to determine concentration of a substance (analyte) in an unknown sample by comparison to a set of samples of known concentration, similar to using a calibration curve. Standard addition can be applied to most analytical techniques and is used instead of a calibration curve to solve the matrix effect problem.

Signals and noise

One of the most important components of analytical chemistry is maximizing the desired signal while minimizing the associated noise. The analytical figure of merit is known as the signal-to-noise ratio (S/N or SNR).

Noise can arise from environmental factors as well as from fundamental physical processes.

Thermal noise

Thermal noise results from the motion of charge carriers (usually electrons) in an electrical circuit generated by their thermal motion. Thermal noise is white noise meaning that the power spectral density is constant throughout the frequency spectrum.

The root mean square value of the thermal noise in a resistor is given by

$$v_{RMS} = \sqrt{4k_B T R \Delta f}$$

where k_B is Boltzmann's constant, T is the temperature, R is the resistance, and Δf is the bandwidth of the frequency f.

Shot noise

Shot noise is a type of electronic noise that occurs when the finite number of particles (such as electrons in an electronic circuit or photons in an optical device) is small enough to give rise to statistical fluctuations in a signal.

Shot noise is a Poisson process and the charge carriers that make up the current follow a Poisson distribution. The root mean square current fluctuation is given by

$$i_{RMS} = \sqrt{2eI\Delta f}$$

where e is the elementary charge and I is the average current. Shot noise is white noise.

Flicker noise

Flicker noise is electronic noise with a $1/f$ frequency spectrum; as f increases, the noise decreases. Flicker noise arises from a variety of sources, such as impurities in a conductive channel, generation and recombination noise in a transistor due to base current, and so on. This noise can be avoided by modulation of the signal at a higher frequency, for example through the use of a lock-in amplifier.

Environmental noise

Noise in a thermogravimetric analysis; lower noise in the middle of the plot results from less human activity (and environmental noise) at night.

Environmental noise arises from the surroundings of the analytical instrument. Sources of electromagnetic noise are power lines, radio and television stations, wireless devices, Compact fluorescent lamps and electric motors. Many of these noise sources are narrow bandwidth and therefore can be avoided. Temperature and vibration isolation may be required for some instruments.

Noise reduction

Noise reduction can be accomplished either in computer hardware or software. Examples of hardware noise reduction are the use of shielded cable, analog filtering, and signal modulation. Examples of software noise reduction are digital filtering, ensemble average, boxcar average, and correlation methods.

Applications

Analytical chemistry research is largely driven by performance (sensitivity, selectivity, robustness, linear range, accuracy, precision, and speed), and cost (purchase, operation, training, time, and space). Among the main branches of contemporary analytical atomic spectrometry, the most widespread and universal are optical and mass spectrometry. In the direct elemental analysis of solid samples, the new leaders are laser-induced breakdown and laser ablation mass spectrometry, and the related techniques with transfer of the laser ablation products into inductively coupled plasma. Advances in design of diode lasers and optical parametric oscillators promote developments in fluorescence and ionization spectrometry and also in absorption techniques where uses of optical cavities for increased effective absorption pathlength are expected to expand. The use of plasma-and laser-based methods is increasing. An interest towards absolute (standardless) analysis has revived, particularly in emission spectrometry.

Great effort is put in shrinking the analysis techniques to chip size. Although there are few examples of such systems competitive with traditional analysis techniques, potential advantages include size/portability, speed, and cost. (micro Total Analysis System (μTAS) or Lab-on-a-chip). Microscale chemistry reduces the amounts of chemicals used.

Many developments improve the analysis of biological systems. Examples of rapidly expanding fields in this area are:

Genomics-DNA sequencing and its related research. Genetic fingerprinting and DNA microarray are important tools and research fields.

Proteomics-the analysis of protein concentrations and modifications, especially in response to various stressors, at various developmental stages, or in various parts of the body.

Metabolomics-similar to proteomics, but dealing with metabolites.

Transcriptomics-mRNA and its associated field

Lipidomics-lipids and its associated field

Peptidomics-peptides and its associated field

Metalomics-similar to proteomics and metabolomics, but dealing with metal concentrations and especially with their binding to proteins and other molecules.

Analytical chemistry has played critical roles in the understanding of basic science to a variety of practical applications, such as biomedical applications, environmental monitoring, quality control of industrial manufacturing, forensic science and so on.

The recent developments of computer automation and information technologies have extended analytical chemistry into a number of new biological fields. For example, automated DNA sequencing machines were the basis to complete human genome projects leading to the birth of genomics. Protein identification and peptide sequencing by mass spectrometry opened a new field of proteomics.

Analytical chemistry has been an indispensable area in the development of nanotechnology. Surface characterization instruments, electron microscopes and scanning probe microscopes enables scientists to visualize atomic structures with chemical characterizations.

36 有机化学*

Organic chemistry

From Wikipedia, the free encyclopedia

Methane, CH_4, in line-angle representation, showing four carbon-hydrogen single (σ) bonds in black, and the 3D shape of such tetrahedral molecules, with ~109° interior bond angles, in green. Methane is the simplest organic chemical and simplest hydrocarbon, and molecules can be built up conceptually from it by exchanging up to all 4 hydrogens with carbon or other atoms.

Organic chemistry is a chemistry subdiscipline involving the scientific study of the structure, properties, and reactions of organic compounds and organic materials, i.e., matter in its various forms that contain carbon atoms. Study of structure includes using spectroscopy (e.g., NMR), mass spectrometry, and other physical and chemical methods to determine the chemical composition and constitution of organic compounds and materials. Study of properties includes both physical properties and chemical properties, and uses similar methods as well as methods to evaluate chemical reactivity, with the aim to understand the behavior of the organic matter in its pure form (when possible), but also in solutions, mixtures, and fabricated forms. The study of organic reactions includes probing their scope through use in preparation of target compounds (e.g., natural products, drugs, polymers, etc.) by chemical synthesis, as well as the focused study of the reactivities of individual organic molecules, both in the laboratory and via theoretical (in silico) study.

The range of chemicals studied in organic chemistry include hydrocarbons, compounds containing only carbon and hydrogen, as well as myriad compositions based always on carbon, but also containing other elements, especially: oxygen, nitrogen, sulfur, phosphorus (these, included in many organic chemicals in biology) and the radiostable of the halogens.

In the modern era, the range extends further into the periodic table, with main group elements, including:

Group 1 and 2 organometallic compounds, i. e. , involving alkali (e. g. , lithium, sodium, and potassium) or alkaline earth metals (e. g. , magnesium), or

metalloids (e. g. , boron and silicon) or other metals (e. g. , aluminum and tin).

In addition, much modern research focuses on organic chemistry involving further organometallics, including the lanthanides, but especially the:

transition metals (e. g. , zinc, copper, palladium, nickel, cobalt, titanium, chromium, etc.).

Three representations of an organic compound, 5α-Dihydroprogesterone (5α-DHP), a steroid hormone. For molecules showing color, the carbon atoms are in black, hydrogens in gray, and oxygens in red. In the line angle representation, carbon atoms are implied at every terminus of a line and vertex of multiple lines, and hydrogen atoms are implied to fill the remaining needed valences (up to 4).

Finally, organic compounds form the basis of all earthly life and constitute a significant part of human endeavors in chemistry. The bonding patterns open to carbon, with its valence of four formal single, double, and triple bonds, as well as various structures with delocalized electrons-make the array of organic compounds structurally diverse, and their range of applications enormous. They either form the basis of, or are important constituents of, many commercial products including pharmaceuticals, supplements, and foods; petrochemicals and products made from them, including lubricants, solvents, paints, and plastics; fuels and explosives; etc. As indicated, the study of organic chemistry overlaps with organometallic chemistry and biochemistry, but also with medicinal chemistry, polymer chemistry, as well as many aspects of materials science.

Contents

1 History
2 Characterization
3 Properties
   3. 1 Melting and boiling properties
   3. 2 Solubility
   3. 3 Solid state properties

4 Nomenclature
    4.1 Structural drawings
5 Classification of organic compounds
    5.1 Functional groups
    5.2 Aliphatic compounds
    5.3 Aromatic compounds
    5.3.1 Heterocyclic compounds
    5.4 Polymers
    5.5 Biomolecules
    5.6 Small molecules
    5.7 Fullerenes
    5.8 Others
6 Organic synthesis
7 Organic reactions
8 See also
9 References
10 External links

History

Before the nineteenth century, chemists generally believed that compounds obtained from living organisms were endowed with a vital force that distinguished them from inorganic compounds. According to the concept of vitalism (vital force theory), organic matter was endowed with a "vital force". During the first half of the nineteenth century, some of the first systematic studies of organic compounds were reported. Around 1816 Michel Chevreul started a study of soaps made from various fats and alkalis. He separated the different acids that, in combination with the alkali, produced the soap. Since these were all individual compounds, he demonstrated that it was possible to make a chemical change in various fats (which traditionally come from organic sources), producing new compounds, without "vital force". In 1828 Friedrich Wöhler produced the organic chemical urea (carbamide), a constituent of urine, from the inorganic ammonium cyanate NH_4CNO, in what is now called the Wöhler synthesis. Although Wöhler was always cautious about claiming that he had disproved the theory of vital force, this event has often been thought of as a turning point.

In 1856 William Henry Perkin, while trying to manufacture quinine, accidentally manufactured the organic dye now known as Perkin's mauve. Through its great financial success, this discovery greatly increased interest in organic chemistry.

The crucial breakthrough for organic chemistry was the concept of chemical structure, developed independently and simultaneously by Friedrich August Kekulé and Archibald Scott Couper in 1858. Both men suggested that tetravalent carbon atoms could link to each other to form a carbon lattice, and that the detailed patterns of atomic bonding could be discerned by skillful interpretations of appropriate chemical reactions.

The pharmaceutical industry began in the last decade of the 19th century when the manufacturing of acetylsalicylic acid (more commonly referred to as aspirin) in Germany was started by Bayer. The first time a drug was systematically improved was with arsphenamine (Salvarsan). Though numerous derivatives of the dangerous toxic atoxyl were examined by Paul Ehrlich and his group, the compound with best effectiveness and toxicity characteristics was selected for production.

Early examples of organic reactions and applications were often serendipitous. The latter half of the 19th century however witnessed systematic studies of organic compounds, Illustrative is the development of synthetic indigo. The production of indigo from plant sources dropped from 19 000 tons in 1897 to 1 000 tons by 1914 thanks to the synthetic methods developed by Adolf von Baeyer. In 2002, 17 000 tons of synthetic indigo were produced from petrochemicals.

In the early part of the 20th Century, polymers and enzymes were shown to be large organic molecules, and petroleum was shown to be of biological origin.

The multistep synthesis of complex organic compounds is called total synthesis. Total synthesis of complex natural compounds increased in complexity to glucose and terpineol. For example, cholesterol-related compounds have opened ways to synthesize complex human hormones and their modified derivatives. Since the start of the 20th century, complexity of total syntheses has been increased to include molecules of high complexity such as lysergic acid and vitamin B12.

The development of organic chemistry benefited from the discovery of petroleum and the development of the petrochemical industry. The conversion of individual compounds obtained from petroleum into different compound types by various chemical processes led to the birth of the petrochemical industry, which successfully manufactured artificial rubbers, various organic adhesives, property-modifying petroleum additives, and plastics.

The majority of chemical compounds occurring in biological organisms are in fact carbon compounds, so the association between organic chemistry and biochemistry is so close that biochemistry might be regarded as in essence a branch of organic chemistry. Although the history of biochemistry might be taken to span some four centuries, fundamental understanding of the field only began to develop in the late 19th century and the actual term biochemistry was coined around the start of 20th century. Research in the field increased throughout the twentieth century, without any indication of slackening in the rate of increase, as may be verified by inspection of abstraction and indexing services such as BIOSIS Previews and Biological Abstracts, which began in the 1920s as a single annual volume, but has grown so drastically that by the end of the 20th century it was only available to the everyday user as an online electronic database.

Characterization

Since organic compounds often exist as mixtures, a variety of techniques have also been developed to assess purity, especially important being chromatography techniques such as HPLC and gas chromatography. Traditional methods of separation include distillation, crystallization, and solvent extraction.

Organic compounds were traditionally characterized by a variety of chemical tests, called "wet methods", but such tests have been largely displaced by spectroscopic or other computer-intensive methods of analysis. Listed in approximate order of utility, the chief analytical methods are:

Nuclear magnetic resonance (NMR) spectroscopy is the most commonly used technique, often permitting complete assignment of atom connectivity and even stereochemistry using correlation spectroscopy. The principal constituent atoms of organic chemistry-hydrogen and carbon-exist naturally with NMR-responsive isotopes, respectively ^1H and ^{13}C.

Elemental analysis: A destructive method used to determine the elemental composition of a molecule. See also mass spectrometry, below.

Mass spectrometry indicates the molecular weight of a compound and, from the fragmentation patterns, its structure. High resolution mass spectrometry can usually identify the exact formula of a compound and is used in lieu of elemental analysis. In former times, mass spectrometry was restricted to neutral molecules exhibiting some volatility, but advanced ionization techniques allow one to obtain the "mass spec" of virtually any organic compound.

Crystallography is an unambiguous method for determining molecular geometry, the proviso being that single crystals of the material must be available and the crystal must be representative of the sample. Highly automated software allows a structure to be determined within hours of obtaining a suitable crystal.

Traditional spectroscopic methods such as infrared spectroscopy, optical rotation, UV/VIS spectroscopy provide relatively nonspecific structural information but remain in use for specific classes of compounds.

Properties

Physical properties of organic compounds typically of interest include both quantitative and qualitative features. Quantitative information includes melting point, boiling point, and index of refraction. Qualitative properties include odor, consistency, solubility, and color.

Melting and boiling properties

Organic compounds typically melt and many boil. In contrast, while inorganic materials generally can be melted, many do not boil, tending instead to degrade. In earlier times, the melting point (m. p.) and boiling point (b. p.) provided crucial information on the purity and identity of organic compounds. The melting and boiling points correlate with the polarity of the molecules and their molecular weight. Some organic compounds, especially symmetrical ones, sublime, that is they evaporate without melting. A well-known example of a sublimable organic compound is para-dichlorobenzene, the odiferous constituent of modern mothballs. Organic compounds are usually not very stable at temperatures above 300 °C, although some exceptions exist.

Solubility

Neutral organic compounds tend to be hydrophobic; that is, they are less soluble in water than in organic solvents. Exceptions include organic compounds that contain ionizable groups as well as low molecular weight alcohols, amines, and carboxylic acids where hydrogen bonding occurs. Organic compounds tend to dissolve in organic solvents. Solvents can be either pure substances like ether or ethyl alcohol, or mixtures, such as the paraffinic solvents such as the various petroleum ethers and white spirits, or the range of pure or mixed aromatic solvents obtained from petroleum or tar fractions by physical separation or by chemical conversion. Solubility in the different solvents depends upon the solvent type and on the functional groups if present.

Solid state properties

Various specialized properties of molecular crystals and organic polymers with conjugated systems are of interest depending on applications, e. g. thermo-mechanical and electro-mechanical such as piezoelectricity, electrical conductivity (see conductive polymers and organic semiconductors), and electro-optical (e. g. non-linear optics) properties. For historical reasons, such properties are mainly the subjects of the areas of polymer science and materials science.

Polymers

One important property of carbon is that it readily forms chains, or networks, that are linked by carbon-carbon (carbon to carbon) bonds. The linking process is called polymerization, while the chains, or networks, are called polymers. The source compound is called a monomer.

Two main groups of polymers exist: synthetic polymers and biopolymers. Synthetic polymers are artificially manufactured, and are commonly referred to as industrial polymers. Biopolymers occur within a respectfully natural environment, or without human intervention.

Since the invention of the first synthetic polymer product, bakelite, synthetic polymer products have frequently been invented.

Common synthetic organic polymers are polyethylene (polythene), polypropylene, nylon, teflon (PTFE), polystyrene, polyesters, polymethylmethacrylate (called perspex and plexiglas), and polyvinylchloride (PVC).

Both synthetic and natural rubber are polymers.

Varieties of each synthetic polymer product may exist, for purposes of a specific use. Changing the conditions of polymerization alters the chemical composition of the product and its properties. These alterations include the chain length, or branching, or the tacticity.

With a single monomer as a start, the product is a homopolymer.

Secondary component(s) may be added to create a heteropolymer (co-polymer) and the degree of clustering of the different components can also be controlled.

Physical characteristics, such as hardness, density, mechanical or tensile strength, abrasion resistance, heat resistance, transparency, colour, etc. will depend on the final composition.

Biomolecules

Biomolecular chemistry is a major category within organic chemistry which is frequently studied by biochemists. Many complex multi-functional group molecules are important in living organisms. Some are long-chain biopolymers, and these include peptides, DNA, RNA and the polysaccharides such as starches in animals and celluloses in plants. The other main classes are amino acids (monomer building blocks of peptides and proteins), carbohydrates (which includes the polysaccharides), the nucleic acids (which include DNA and RNA as polymers), and the lipids. In addition, animal biochemistry contains many small molecule intermediates which assist in energy production through the Krebs cycle, and produces isoprene, the most common hydrocarbon in animals. Isoprenes in animals form the important steroid structural (cholesterol) and steroid hormone compounds; and in plants form terpenes, terpenoids, some alkaloids, and a class of hydrocarbons called biopolymer polyisoprenoids present in the latex of various species of plants, which is the basis for making rubber.

Small molecules

In pharmacology, an important group of organic compounds is small molecules, also referred to as 'small organic compounds'. In this context, a small molecule is a small organic compound that is biologically active, but is not a polymer.

In practice, small molecules have a molar mass less than approximately 1 000 g/mol.

Organic synthesis

Synthetic organic chemistry is an applied science as it borders engineering, the "design, analysis, and/or construction of works for practical purposes". Organic synthesis of a novel compound is a problem solving task, where a synthesis is designed for a target molecule by selecting optimal reactions from optimal starting materials. Complex compounds can have tens of reaction steps that sequentially build the desired molecule. The synthesis proceeds by utilizing the reactivity of the functional groups in the molecule. For example, a carbonyl compound can be used as a nucleophile by converting it into an enolate, or as an electrophile; the combination of the two is called the aldol reaction. Designing practically useful syntheses always requires conducting the actual synthesis in the laboratory. The scientific practice of creating novel synthetic routes for complex molecules is called total synthesis.

Strategies to design a synthesis include retrosynthesis, popularized by E. J. Corey, starts with the target molecule and splices it to pieces according to known reactions. The pieces, or the proposed precursors, receive the same treatment, until available and ideally inexpensive starting materials are reached. Then, the retrosynthesis is written in the opposite direction to give the synthesis. A "synthetic tree" can be constructed, because each compound and also each precursor has multiple syntheses.

Organic reactions

Organic reactions are chemical reactions involving organic compounds. Many of these reactions are associated with functional groups. The general theory of these reactions involves careful analysis of such properties as the electron affinity of key atoms, bond strengths and steric hindrance. These factors can determine the relative stability of short-lived reactive intermediates, which usually directly determine the path of the reaction.

The basic reaction types are: addition reactions, elimination reactions, substitution reactions, pericyclic reactions, rearrangement reactions and redox reactions. An example of a common reaction is a substitution reaction written as:

$$Nu^- + C-X \rightarrow C-Nu + X^-$$

where X is some functional group and Nu is a nucleophile.

The number of possible organic reactions is basically infinite. However, certain general patterns are observed that can be used to describe many common or useful reactions. Each reaction has a stepwise reaction mechanism that explains how it happens in sequence-although the detailed description of steps is not always clear from a list of reactants alone.

The stepwise course of any given reaction mechanism can be represented using arrow pushing techniques in which curved arrows are used to track the movement of electrons as starting materials transition through intermediates to final products.

37　物理化学*

Physical chemistry

From Wikipedia, the free encyclopedia

Physical chemistry is the study of macroscopic, atomic, subatomic, and particulate phenomena in chemical systems in terms of laws and concepts of physics. It applies the principles, practices and concepts of physics such as motion, energy, force, time, thermodynamics, quantum chemistry, statistical mechanics and dynamics, equilibrium.

Physical chemistry, in contrast to chemical physics, is predominantly (but not always) a macroscopic or supra-molecular science, as the majority of the principles on which physical chemistry was founded, are concepts related to the bulk rather than on molecular/atomic structure alone. For example, chemical equilibrium, and colloids.

Some of the relationships that physical chemistry strives to resolve include the effects of:

Intermolecular forces that act upon the physical properties of materials (plasticity, tensile strength, surface tension in liquids).

Reaction kinetics on the rate of a reaction.

The identity of ions and the electrical conductivity of materials.

Surface chemistry and electrochemistry of membranes.

Interaction of one body with another in terms of quantities of heat and work called thermodynamics.

Transfer of heat between a chemical system and its surroundings during change of phase or chemical reaction taking place called thermochemistry

Study of colligative properties of number of species present in solution.

Number of phases, number of components and degree of freedom (or variance) can be correlated with one another with help of phase rule.

Reactions of electrochemical cells.

Contents

1 Key concepts
2 History
3 Journals
4 Branches and related topics
5 See also
6 References
7 External links

Key concepts

The key concepts of physical chemistry are the ways in which pure physics is applied to chemical problems.

One of the key concepts in classical chemistry is that all chemical compounds can be described as groups of atoms bonded together and chemical reactions can be described as the making and breaking of those bonds. Predicting the properties of chemical compounds from a description of atoms and how they bond is one of the major goals of physical chemistry. To describe the atoms and bonds precisely, it is necessary to know both where the nuclei of the atoms are, and how electrons are distributed around them.

Quantum chemistry, a subfield of physical chemistry especially concerned with the application of quantum mechanics to chemical problems, provides tools to determine how strong and what shape bonds are, how nuclei move, and how light can be absorbed or emitted by a chemical compound. Spectroscopy is the related sub-discipline of physical chemistry which is specifically concerned with the interaction of electromagnetic radiation with matter.

Another set of important questions in chemistry concerns what kind of reactions can happen spontaneously and which properties are possible for a given chemical mixture. This is studied in chemical thermodynamics, which sets limits on quantities like how far a reaction can proceed, or how much energy can be converted into work in an internal combustion engine, and which provides links between properties like the thermal expansion coefficient and rate of change of entropy with pressure for a gas or a liquid. It can frequently be used to assess whether a reactor or engine design is feasible, or to check the validity of experimental data. To a limited extent, quasi-equilibrium and non-equilibrium thermodynamics can describe irreversible changes. However, classical thermodynamics is mostly concerned with systems in equilibrium and reversible changes and not what actually does happen, or how fast, away from equilibrium.

Which reactions do occur and how fast is the subject of chemical kinetics, another branch of physical chemistry. A key idea in chemical kinetics is that for reactants to react and form products, most chemical species must go through transition states which are higher in energy than either the reactants or the products and serve as a barrier to reaction. In general, the higher the barrier, the slower the reaction. A second is that most chemical reactions occur as a sequence of elementary reactions, each with its own transition state. Key questions in kinetics include how the rate of reaction depends on temperature and on the concentrations of reactants and catalysts in the reaction mixture, as well as how catalysts and reaction conditions can be engineered to optimize the reaction rate.

The fact that how fast reactions occur can often be specified with just a few concentrations and a temperature, instead of needing to know all the positions and speeds of every molecule in a mixture, is a special case of another key concept in physical chemistry, which is that to the extent an engineer needs to know, everything going on in a mixture of very large numbers (perhaps of the order of the Avogadro constant, 6×10^{23}) of particles can often be described by just a few variables like pressure, temperature, and concentration. The precise reasons for this are described in statistical mechanics, a specialty within physical chemistry which is also shared with physics. Statistical mechanics also provides ways to predict the properties we see in everyday life from molecular properties without relying on empirical correlations based on chemical similarities.

History

The term "physical chemistry" was coined by Mikhail Lomonosov in 1752, when he presented a lecture course entitled "A Course in True Physical Chemistry" (Russian: 《Курс истинной физической химии》) before the students of Petersburg University. In the preamble to these lectures he gives definition: "Physical chemistry is the science that must explain under provisions of physical experiments the reason for what is happening in complex bodies through chemical operations".

Modern physical chemistry originated in the 1860s to 1880s with work on chemical thermodynamics, electrolytes in solutions, chemical kinetics and other subjects. One milestone was the publication in 1876 by Josiah Willard Gibbs of his paper, On the Equilibrium of Heterogeneous Substances. This paper introduced several of the cornerstones of physical chemistry, such as Gibbs energy, chemical potentials, Gibbs phase rule. Other milestones include the subsequent naming and accreditation of enthalpy to Heike Kamerlingh Onnes and to macromolecular processes.

The first scientific journal specifically in the field of physical chemistry was the German journal, Zeitschrift für Physikalische Chemie, founded in 1887 by Wilhelm Ostwald and Jacobus Henricus van't Hoff. Together with Svante August Arrhenius, these were the leading figures in physical chemistry in the late 19th century and early 20th century. All three were awarded with the Nobel Prize in Chemistry between 1901—1909.

Developments in the following decades include the application of statistical mechanics to chemical systems and work on colloids and surface chemistry, where Irving Langmuir made many contributions. Another important step was the development of quantum mechanics into quantum chemistry from the 1930s, where Linus Pauling was one of the leading names. Theoretical developments have gone hand in hand with developments in experimental methods, where the use of different forms of spectroscopy, such as infrared spectroscopy, microwave spectroscopy, EPR spectroscopy and NMR spectroscopy, is probably the most important 20th century development.

Further development in physical chemistry may be attributed to discoveries in nuclear chemistry, especially in isotope separation (before and during World War II), more recent discoveries in astrochemistry, as well as the development of calculation algorithms in the field of "additive physicochemical properties" (practically all physicochemical properties, such as boiling point, critical point, surface tension, vapor pressure, etc. -more than 20 in all-can be precisely calculated from chemical structure alone, even if the chemical molecule remains unsynthesized), and in this area is concentrated practical importance of contemporary physical chemistry.

38 纳米技术*

Nanotechnology

From Wikipedia, the free encyclopedia

Nanotechnology (sometimes shortened to "nanotech") is the manipulation of matter on an atomic, molecular, and supramolecular scale. The earliest, widespread description of nanotechnology referred to the particular technological goal of precisely manipulating atoms and molecules for fabrication of macroscale products, also now referred to as molecular nanotechnology. A more generalized description of nanotechnology was subsequently established by the National Nanotechnology Initiative, which defines nanotechnology as the manipulation of matter with at least one dimension sized from 1 to 100 nanometers. This definition reflects the fact that quantum mechanical effects are important at this quantum-realm scale, and so the definition shifted from a particular technological goal to a research category inclusive of all types of research and technologies that deal with the special properties of matter that occur below the given size threshold. It is therefore common to see the plural form "nanotechnologies" as well as "nanoscale technologies" to refer to the broad range of research and applications whose common trait is size. Because of the variety of potential applications (including industrial and military), governments have invested billions of dollars in nanotechnology research. Through its National Nanotechnology Initiative, the USA has invested 3.7 billion dollars. The European Union has invested 1.2 billion and Japan 750 million dollars.

Nanotechnology as defined by size is naturally very broad, including fields of science as diverse as surface science, organic chemistry, molecular biology, semiconductor physics, microfabrication, etc. The associated research and applications are equally diverse, ranging from extensions of conventional device physics to completely new approaches based upon molecular self-assembly, from developing new materials with dimensions on the nanoscale to direct control of matter on the atomic scale.

Scientists currently debate the future implications of nanotechnology. Nanotechnology may be able to create many new materials and devices with a vast range of applications, such as in medicine, electronics, biomaterials and energy production. On the other hand, nanotechnology raises many of the same issues as any new technology, including concerns about the toxicity and environmental impact of nanomaterials, and their potential effects on global economics, as well as speculation about various doomsday scenarios. These concerns have led to a debate among advocacy groups and governments on whether special regulation of nanotechnology is warranted.

Contents

1 Origins
2 Fundamental concepts
    2.1 Larger to smaller: a materials perspective
    2.2 Simple to complex: a molecular perspective
    2.3 Molecular nanotechnology: a long—term view
3 Current research
    3.1 Nanomaterials
    3.2 Bottom-up approaches
    3.3 Top-down approaches
    3.4 Functional approaches
    3.5 Biomimetic approaches
    3.6 Speculative
4 Tools and techniques
5 Applications
6 Implications
    6.1 Health and environmental concerns
7 Regulation
8 See also
9 References
10 External links

Origins

The concepts that seeded nanotechnology were first discussed in 1959 by renowned physicist Richard Feynman in his talk There's Plenty of Room at the Bottom, in which he described the possibility of synthesis via direct manipulation of atoms. The term "nano-technology" was first used by Norio Taniguchi in 1974, though it was not widely known.

Inspired by Feynman's concepts, K. Eric Drexler independently used the term "nanotechnology" in his 1986 book Engines of Creation: The Coming Era of Nanotechnology, which proposed the idea of a nanoscale "assembler" which would be able to build a copy of itself and of other items of arbitrary complexity with atomic control. Also in 1986, Drexler co-founded The Foresight Institute (with which he is no longer affiliated) to help increase public awareness and understanding of nanotechnology concepts and implications.

Thus, emergence of nanotechnology as a field in the 1980s occurred through convergence of Drexler's theoretical and public work, which developed and popularized a conceptual framework for nanotechnology, and high-visibility experimental advances that drew additional wide-scale attention to the prospects of atomic control of matter.

For example, the invention of the scanning tunneling microscope in 1981 provided unprecedented visualization of individual atoms and bonds, and was successfully used to manipulate individual atoms in 1989. The microscope's developers Gerd Binnig and Heinrich Rohrer at IBM Zurich Research Laboratory received a Nobel Prize in Physics in 1986. Binnig, Quate and Gerber also invented the analogous atomic force microscope that year.

Fullerenes were discovered in 1985 by Harry Kroto, Richard Smalley, and Robert Curl, who together won the 1996 Nobel Prize in Chemistry. C_{60} was not initially described as nanotechnology; the term was used regarding subsequent work with related graphene tubes (called carbon nanotubes and sometimes called Bucky tubes) which suggested potential applications for nanoscale electronics and devices.

In the early 2000s, the field garnered increased scientific, political, and commercial attention that led to both controversy and progress. Controversies emerged regarding the definitions and potential implications of nanotechnologies, exemplified by the Royal Society's report on nanotechnology. Challenges were raised regarding the feasibility of applications envisioned by advocates of molecular nanotechnology, which culminated in a public debate between Drexler and Smalley in 2001 and 2003.

Meanwhile, commercialization of products based on advancements in nanoscale technologies began emerging. These products are limited to bulk applications of nanomaterials and do not involve atomic control of matter. Some examples include the Silver Nano platform for using silver nanoparticles as an antibacterial agent, nanoparticle-based transparent sunscreens, and carbon nanotubes for stain-resistant textiles.

Governments moved to promote and fund research into nanotechnology, beginning in the U. S. with the National Nanotechnology Initiative, which formalized a size-based definition of nanotechnology and established funding for research on the nanoscale.

By the mid-2000s new and serious scientific attention began to flourish. Projects emerged to produce nanotechnology roadmaps which center on atomically precise manipulation of matter and discuss existing and projected capabilities, goals, and applications.

Fundamental concepts

Nanotechnology is the engineering of functional systems at the molecular scale. This covers both current work and concepts that are more advanced. In its original sense, nanotechnology refers to the projected ability to construct items from the bottom up, using techniques and tools being developed today to make complete, high performance products.

One nanometer (nm) is one billionth, or 10^{-9}, of a meter. By comparison, typical carbon-carbon bond lengths, or the spacing between these atoms in a molecule, are in the range 0.12~0.15 nm, and a DNA double-helix has a diameter around 2 nm. On the other hand, the smallest cellular life-forms, the bacteria of the genus Mycoplasma, are around 200 nm in length. By convention, nanotechnology is taken as the scale range 1 to 100 nm following the definition used by the National Nanotechnology Initiative in the US. The lower limit is set by the size of atoms (hydrogen has the smallest atoms, which are approximately a quarter of a nm diameter) since nanotechnology must build its devices from atoms and molecules. The upper limit is more or less arbitrary but is around the size that phenomena not observed in larger structures start to become apparent and can be made use of in the nano device. These new phenomena make nanotechnology distinct from devices which are merely miniaturised versions of an equivalent macroscopic device; such devices are on a larger scale and come under the description of microtechnology.

To put that scale in another context, the comparative size of a nanometer to a meter is the same as that of a marble to the size of the earth. Or another way of putting it: a nanometer is the amount an average man's beard grows in the time it takes him to raise the razor to his face.

Two main approaches are used in nanotechnology. In the "bottom-up" approach, materials and devices are built from molecular components which assemble themselves chemically by principles of molecular recognition. In the "top-down" approach, nano-objects are constructed from larger entities without atomic-level control.

Areas of physics such as nanoelectronics, nanomechanics, nanophotonics and nanoionics have evolved during the last few decades to provide a basic scientific foundation of nanotechnology.

Larger to smaller: a materials perspective

Several phenomena become pronounced as the size of the system decreases. These include statistical mechanical effects, as well as quantum mechanical effects, for example the "quantum size effect" where the electronic properties of solids are altered with great reductions in particle size. This effect does not come into play by going from macro to micro dimensions. However, quantum effects can become significant when the nanometer size range is reached, typically at distances of 100 nanometers or less, the so-called quantum realm. Additionally, a number of physical (mechanical, electrical, optical, etc.) properties change when compared to macroscopic systems. One example is the increase in surface area to volume ratio altering mechanical, thermal and catalytic properties of materials. Diffusion and reactions at nanoscale, nanostructures materials and nanodevices with fast ion transport are generally referred to nanoionics. Mechanical properties of nanosystems are of interest in the nanomechanics research. The catalytic activity of nanomaterials also opens potential risks in their interaction with biomaterials.

Materials reduced to the nanoscale can show different properties compared to what they exhibit on a macroscale, enabling unique applications. For instance, opaque substances can become transparent (copper); stable materials can turn combustible (aluminum); insoluble materials may become soluble (gold). A material such as gold, which is chemically inert at normal scales, can serve as a potent chemical catalyst at nanoscales. Much of the fascination with nanotechnology stems from these quantum and surface phenomena that matter exhibits at the nanoscale.

Simple to complex: a molecular perspective

Modern synthetic chemistry has reached the point where it is possible to prepare small molecules to almost any structure. These methods are used today to manufacture a wide variety of useful chemicals such as pharmaceuticals or commercial polymers. This ability raises the question of extending this kind of control to the next-larger level, seeking methods to assemble these single molecules into supramolecular assemblies consisting of many molecules arranged in a well defined manner.

These approaches utilize the concepts of molecular self-assembly and/or supramolecular chemistry to automatically arrange themselves into some useful conformation through a bottom-up approach. The concept of molecular recognition is especially important: molecules can be designed so that a specific configuration or arrangement is favored due to non-covalent intermolecular forces. The Watson-Crick basepairing rules are a direct result of this, as is the specificity of an enzyme being targeted to a single substrate, or the specific folding of the protein itself. Thus, two or more components can be designed to be complementary and mutually attractive so that they make a more complex and useful whole.

Such bottom-up approaches should be capable of producing devices in parallel and be much cheaper than top-down methods, but could potentially be overwhelmed as the size and complexity of the desired assembly increases. Most useful structures require complex and thermodynamically unlikely arrangements of atoms. Nevertheless, there are many examples of self-assembly based on molecular recognition in biology, most notably Watson-Crick basepairing and enzyme-substrate interactions. The challenge for nanotechnology is whether these principles can be used to engineer new constructs in addition to natural ones.

Molecular nanotechnology: a long-term view

Molecular nanotechnology, sometimes called molecular manufacturing, describes engineered nanosystems (nanoscale machines) operating on the molecular scale. Molecular nanotechnology is especially associated with the molecular assembler, a machine that can produce a desired structure or device atom-by-atom using the principles of mechanosynthesis. Manufacturing in the context of productive nanosystems is not related to, and should be clearly distinguished from, the conventional technologies used to manufacture nanomaterials such as carbon nanotubes and nanoparticles.

When the term "nanotechnology" was independently coined and popularized by Eric Drexler (who at the time was unaware of an earlier usage by Norio Taniguchi) it referred to a future manufacturing technology based on molecular machine systems. The premise was that molecular scale biological analogies of traditional machine components demonstrated molecular machines were possible: by the countless examples found in biology, it is known that sophisticated, stochastically optimised biological machines can be produced.

It is hoped that developments in nanotechnology will make possible their construction by some other means, perhaps using biomimetic principles. However, Drexler and other researchers have proposed that advanced nanotechnology, although perhaps initially implemented by biomimetic means, ultimately could be based on mechanical engineering principles, namely, a manufacturing technology based on the mechanical functionality of these components (such as gears, bearings, motors, and structural members) that would enable programmable, positional assembly to atomic specification. The physics and engineering performance of exemplar designs were analyzed in Drexler's book Nanosystems.

In general it is very difficult to assemble devices on the atomic scale, as one has to position atoms on other atoms of comparable size and stickiness. Another view, put forth by Carlo Montemagno, is that future nanosystems will be hybrids of silicon technology and biological molecular machines. Richard Smalley argued that mechanosynthesis are impossible due to the difficulties in mechanically manipulating individual molecules.

This led to an exchange of letters in the ACS publication Chemical & Engineering News in 2003. Though biology clearly demonstrates that molecular machine systems are possible, non-biological molecular machines are today only in their infancy. Leaders in research on non-biological molecular machines are Dr. Alex Zettl and his colleagues at Lawrence Berkeley Laboratories and UC Berkeley. They have constructed at least three distinct molecular devices whose motion is controlled from the desktop with changing voltage: a nanotube nanomotor, a molecular actuator, and a nanoelectromechanical relaxation oscillator. See nanotube nanomotor for more examples.

An experiment indicating that positional molecular assembly is possible was performed by Ho and Lee at Cornell University in 1999. They used a scanning tunneling microscope to move an individual carbon monoxide molecule (CO) to an individual iron atom (Fe) sitting on a flat silver crystal, and chemically bound the CO to the Fe by applying a voltage.

Current research

Nanomaterials

The nanomaterials field includes subfields which develop or study materials having unique properties arising from their nanoscale dimensions.

Interface and colloid science has given rise to many materials which may be useful in nanotechnology, such as carbon nanotubes and other fullerenes, and various nanoparticles and nanorods. Nanomaterials with fast ion transport are related also to nanoionics and nanoelectronics.

Nanoscale materials can also be used for bulk applications; most present commercial applications of nanotechnology are of this flavor.

Progress has been made in using these materials for medical applications; see Nanomedicine.

Nanoscale materials such as nanopillars are sometimes used in solar cells which combats the cost of traditional Silicon solar cells.

Development of applications incorporating semiconductor nanoparticles to be used in the next generation of products, such as display technology, lighting, solar cells and biological imaging; see quantum dots.

Bottom-up approaches

These seek to arrange smaller components into more complex assemblies.

DNA nanotechnology utilizes the specificity of Watson-Crick basepairing to construct well-defined structures out of DNA and other nucleic acids.

Approaches from the field of "classical" chemical synthesis (inorganic and organic synthesis) also aim at designing molecules with well-defined shape (e. g. bis-peptides).

More generally, molecular self-assembly seeks to use concepts of supramolecular chemistry, and molecular recognition in particular, to cause single-molecule components to automatically arrange themselves into some useful conformation.

Atomic force microscope tips can be used as a nanoscale "write head" to deposit a chemical upon a surface in a desired pattern in a process called dip pen nanolithography. This technique fits into the larger subfield of nanolithography.

Top-down approaches

These seek to create smaller devices by using larger ones to direct their assembly.

Many technologies that descended from conventional solid-state silicon methods for fabricating microprocessors are now capable of creating features smaller than 100 nm, falling under the definition of nanotechnology. Giant magnetoresistance-based hard drives already on the market fit this description, as do atomic layer deposition (ALD) techniques. Peter Grünberg and Albert Fert received the Nobel Prize in Physics in 2007 for their discovery of Giant magnetoresistance and contributions to the field of spintronics.

Solid-state techniques can also be used to create devices known as nanoelectromechanical systems or NEMS, which are related to microelectromechanical systems or MEMS.

Focused ion beams can directly remove material, or even deposit material when suitable precursor gasses are applied at the same time. For example, this technique is used routinely to create sub-100 nm sections of material for analysis in Transmission electron microscopy.

Atomic force microscope tips can be used as a nanoscale "write head" to deposit a resist, which is then followed by an etching process to remove material in a top-down method.

Functional approaches

These seek to develop components of a desired functionality without regard to how they might be assembled.

Molecular scale electronics seeks to develop molecules with useful electronic properties. These could then be used as single-molecule components in a nanoelectronic device. For an example see rotaxane.

Synthetic chemical methods can also be used to create synthetic molecular motors, such as in a so-called nanocar.

Biomimetic approaches

Bionics or biomimicry seeks to apply biological methods and systems found in nature, to the study and design of engineering systems and modern technology. Biomineralization is one example of the systems studied.

Bionanotechnology is the use of biomolecules for applications in nanotechnology, including use of viruses and lipid assemblies. Nanocellulose is a potential bulk-scale application.

Speculative

These subfields seek to anticipate what inventions nanotechnology might yield, or attempt to propose an agenda along which inquiry might progress. These often take a big-picture view of nanotechnology, with more emphasis on its societal implications than the details of how such inventions could actually be created.

Molecular nanotechnology is a proposed approach which involves manipulating single molecules in finely controlled, deterministic ways. This is more theoretical than the other subfields, and many of its proposed techniques are beyond current capabilities.

Nanorobotics centers on self-sufficient machines of some functionality operating at the nanoscale. There are hopes for applying nanorobots in medicine, but it may not be easy to do such a thing because of several drawbacks of such devices. Nevertheless, progress on innovative materials and methodologies has been demonstrated with some patents granted about new nanomanufacturing devices for future commercial applications, which also progressively helps in the development towards nanorobots with the use of embedded nanobioelectronics concepts.

Productive nanosystems are "systems of nanosystems" which will be complex nanosystems that produce atomically precise parts for other nanosystems, not necessarily using novel nanoscale-emergent properties, but well-understood fundamentals of manufacturing. Because of the discrete (i.e. atomic) nature of matter and the possibility of exponential growth, this stage is seen as the basis of another industrial revolution. Mihail Roco, one of the architects of the USA's National Nanotechnology Initiative, has proposed four states of nanotechnology that seem to parallel the technical progress of the Industrial Revolution, progressing from passive nanostructures to active nanodevices to complex nanomachines and ultimately to productive nanosystems.

Programmable matter seeks to design materials whose properties can be easily, reversibly and externally controlled though a fusion of information science and materials science.

Due to the popularity and media exposure of the term nanotechnology, the words picotechnology and femtotechnology have been coined in analogy to it, although these are only used rarely and informally.

Tools and techniques

Typical AFM setup. A microfabricated cantilever with a sharp tip is deflected by features on a sample surface, much like in a phonograph but on a much smaller scale. A laser beam reflects off the backside of the cantilever into a set of photodetectors, allowing the deflection to be measured and assembled into an image of the surface.

There are several important modern developments. The atomic force microscope (AFM) and the Scanning Tunneling Microscope (STM) are two early versions of scanning probes that launched nanotechnology. There are other types of scanning probe microscopy. Although conceptually similar to the scanning confocal microscope developed by Marvin Minsky in 1961 and the scanning acoustic microscope (SAM) developed by Calvin Quate and coworkers in the 1970s, newer scanning probe microscopes have much higher resolution, since they are not limited by the wavelength of sound or light.

The tip of a scanning probe can also be used to manipulate nanostructures (a process called positional assembly). Feature-oriented scanning methodology suggested by Rostislav Lapshin appears to be a promising way to implement these nanomanipulations in automatic mode. However, this is still a slow process because of low scanning velocity of the microscope.

Various techniques of nanolithography such as optical lithography, X-ray lithography dip pen nanolithography, electron beam lithography or nanoimprint lithography were also developed. Lithography is a top-down fabrication technique where a bulk material is reduced in size to nanoscale pattern.

Another group of nanotechnological techniques include those used for fabrication of nanotubes and nanowires, those used in semiconductor fabrication such as deep ultraviolet lithography, electron beam lithography, focused ion beam machining, nanoimprint lithography, atomic layer deposition, and molecular vapor deposition, and further including molecular self-assembly techniques such as those employing di-block copolymers. The precursors of these techniques preceded the nanotech era, and are extensions in the development of scientific advancements rather than techniques which were devised with the sole purpose of creating nanotechnology and which were results of nanotechnology research.

The top-down approach anticipates nanodevices that must be built piece by piece in stages, much as manufactured items are made. Scanning probe microscopy is an important technique both for characterization and synthesis of nanomaterials. Atomic force microscopes and scanning tunneling microscopes can be used to look at surfaces and to move atoms around. By designing different tips for these microscopes, they can be used for carving out structures on surfaces and to help guide self-assembling structures. By using, for example, feature-oriented scanning approach, atoms or molecules can be moved around on a surface with scanning probe microscopy techniques. At present, it is expensive and time-consuming for mass production but very suitable for laboratory experimentation.

In contrast, bottom-up techniques build or grow larger structures atom by atom or molecule by molecule. These techniques include chemical synthesis, self-assembly and positional assembly. Dual polarisation interferometry is one tool suitable for characterisation of self assembled thin films. Another variation of the bottom-up approach is molecular beam epitaxy or MBE. Researchers at Bell Telephone Laboratories like John R. Arthur, Alfred Y. Cho, and Art C. Gossard developed and implemented MBE as a research tool in the late 1960s and 1970s. Samples made by MBE were key to the discovery of the fractional quantum Hall effect for which the 1998 Nobel Prize in Physics was awarded. MBE allows scientists to lay down atomically precise layers of atoms and, in the process, build up complex structures. Important for research on semiconductors, MBE is also widely used to make samples and devices for the newly emerging field of spintronics.

However, new therapeutic products, based on responsive nanomaterials, such as the ultradeformable, stress-sensitive Transfersome vesicles, are under development and already approved for human use in some countries.

Applications

One of the major applications of nanotechnology is in the area of nanoelectronics with MOSFET's being made of small nanowires $\sim$10 nm in length. Here is a simulation of such a nanowire.

Nanostructures provide this surface with superhydrophobicity, which lets water droplets roll down the inclined plane.

As of August 21, 2008, the Project on Emerging Nanotechnologies estimates that over 800 manufacturer-identified nanotech products are publicly available, with new ones hitting the market at a pace of 3-4 per week. The project lists all of the products in a publicly accessible online database. Most applications are limited to the use of "first generation" passive nanomaterials which includes titanium dioxide in sunscreen, cosmetics, surface coatings, and some food products; Carbon allotropes used to produce gecko tape; silver in food packaging, clothing, disinfectants and household appliances; zinc oxide in sunscreens and cosmetics, surface coatings, paints and outdoor furniture varnishes; and cerium oxide as a fuel catalyst.

Further applications allow tennis balls to last longer, golf balls to fly straighter, and even bowling balls to become more durable and have a harder surface. Trousers and socks have been infused with nanotechnology so that they will last longer and keep people cool in the summer. Bandages are being infused with silver nanoparticles to heal cuts faster. Cars are being manufactured with nanomaterials so they may need fewer metals and less fuel to operate in the future. Video game consoles and personal computers may become cheaper, faster, and contain more memory thanks to nanotechnology. Nanotechnology may have the ability to make existing medical applications cheaper and easier to use in places like the general practitioner's office and at home.

The National Science Foundation (a major distributor for nanotechnology research in the United States) funded researcher David Berube to study the field of nanotechnology. His findings are published in the monograph Nano-Hype: The Truth Behind the Nanotechnology Buzz. This study concludes that much of what is sold as "nanotechnology" is in fact a recasting of straightforward materials science, which is leading to a "nanotech industry built solely on selling nanotubes, nanowires, and the like" which will "end up with a few suppliers selling low margin products in huge volumes." Further applications which require actual manipulation or arrangement of nanoscale components await further research. Though technologies branded with the term 'nano' are sometimes little related to and fall far short of the most ambitious and transformative technological goals of the sort in molecular manufacturing proposals, the term still connotes such ideas. According to Berube, there may be a danger that a "nano bubble" will form, or is forming already, from the use of the term by scientists and entrepreneurs to garner funding, regardless of interest in the transformative possibilities of more ambitious and far-sighted work.

Implications

An area of concern is the effect that industrial-scale manufacturing and use of nanomaterials would have on human health and the environment, as suggested by nanotoxicology research. For these reasons, some groups advocate that nanotechnology be regulated by governments. Others counter that overregulation would stifle scientific research and the development of beneficial innovations. Public health research agencies, such as the National Institute for Occupational Safety and Health are actively conducting research on potential health effects stemming from exposures to nanoparticles.

Some nanoparticle products may have unintended consequences. Researchers have discovered that bacteriostatic silver nanoparticles used in socks to reduce foot odor are being released in the wash. These particles are then flushed into the waste water stream and may destroy bacteria which are critical components of natural ecosystems, farms, and waste treatment processes.

Public deliberations on risk perception in the US and UK carried out by the Center for Nanotechnology in Society found that participants were more positive about nanotechnologies for energy applications than for health applications, with health applications raising moral and ethical dilemmas such as cost and availability.

Experts, including director of the Woodrow Wilson Center's Project on Emerging Nanotechnologies David Rejeski, have testified that successful commercialization depends on adequate oversight, risk research strategy, and public engagement. Berkeley, California is currently the only city in the United States to regulate nanotechnology; Cambridge, Massachusetts in 2008 considered enacting a similar law, but ultimately rejected it. Relevant for both research on and application of nanotechnologies, the insurability of nanotechnology is contested. Without state regulation of nanotechnology, the availability of private insurance for potential damages is seen as necessary to ensure that burdens are not socialised implicitly.

Health and environmental concerns

Nanofibers are used in several areas and in different products, in everything from aircraft wings to tennis rackets. Inhaling airborne nanoparticles and nanofibers may lead to a number of pulmonary diseases, e.g. fibrosis. Researchers have found that when rats breathed in nanoparticles, the particles settled in the brain and lungs, which led to significant increases in biomarkers for inflammation and stress response and that nanoparticles induce skin aging through oxidative stress in hairless mice.

A two-year study at UCLA's School of Public Health found lab mice consuming nano-titanium dioxide showed DNA and chromosome damage to a degree "linked to all the big killers of man, namely cancer, heart disease, neurological disease and aging".

A major study published more recently in Nature Nanotechnology suggests some forms of carbon nanotubes-a poster child for the "nanotechnology revolution"-could be as harmful as asbestos if inhaled in sufficient quantities. Anthony

Seaton of the Institute of Occupational Medicine in Edinburgh, Scotland, who contributed to the article on carbon nanotubes said "We know that some of them probably have the potential to cause mesothelioma. So those sorts of materials need to be handled very carefully. " In the absence of specific regulation forthcoming from governments, Paull and Lyons (2008) have called for an exclusion of engineered nanoparticles in food. A newspaper article reports that workers in a paint factory developed serious lung disease and nanoparticles were found in their lungs.

Regulation

Calls for tighter regulation of nanotechnology have occurred alongside a growing debate related to the human health and safety risks of nanotechnology. There is significant debate about who is responsible for the regulation of nanotechnology. Some regulatory agencies currently cover some nanotechnology products and processes (to varying degrees)-by "bolting on" nanotechnology to existing regulations-there are clear gaps in these regimes. Davies (2008) has proposed a regulatory road map describing steps to deal with these shortcomings.

Stakeholders concerned by the lack of a regulatory framework to assess and control risks associated with the release of nanoparticles and nanotubes have drawn parallels with bovine spongiform encephalopathy ("mad cow" disease), thalidomide, genetically modified food, nuclear energy, reproductive technologies, biotechnology, and asbestosis. Dr. Andrew Maynard, chief science advisor to the Woodrow Wilson Center's Project on Emerging Nanotechnologies, concludes that there is insufficient funding for human health and safety research, and as a result there is currently limited understanding of the human health and safety risks associated with nanotechnology. As a result, some academics have called for stricter application of the precautionary principle, with delayed marketing approval, enhanced labelling and additional safety data development requirements in relation to certain forms of nanotechnology.

The Royal Society report identified a risk of nanoparticles or nanotubes being released during disposal, destruction and recycling, and recommended that "manufacturers of products that fall under extended producer responsibility regimes such as end-of-life regulations publish procedures outlining how these materials will be managed to minimize possible human and environmental exposure" (p. xiii). Reflecting the challenges for ensuring responsible life cycle regulation, the Institute for Food and Agricultural Standards has proposed that standards for nanotechnology research and development should be integrated across consumer, worker and environmental standards. They also propose that NGOs and other citizen groups play a meaningful role in the development of these standards.

The Center for Nanotechnology in Society has found that people respond to nanotechnologies differently, depending on application-with participants in public deliberations more positive about nanotechnologies for energy than health applications-suggesting that any public calls for nano regulations may differ by technology sector.

39 材料科学*

Materials science

From Wikipedia, the free encyclopedia

Materials science, also commonly known as materials engineering or materials science and engineering, is an interdisciplinary field which deals with the study of matter and their properties; as well as the discovery and design of new materials. This relatively new scientific field involves studying materials through the materials paradigm (synthesis, structure, properties and performance). It incorporates elements of physics and chemistry, and is at the forefront of nanoscience and nanotechnology research. In recent years, materials science has become more widely known as a specific field of science and engineering. It is an important part of forensic engineering (the investigation of materials, products, structures or components that fail or do not operate or function as intended, causing personal injury or damage to property) and failure analysis, the latter being the key to understanding, for example, the cause of various aviation accidents. Many of the most pressing scientific problems that are faced today are due to the limitations of the materials that are available and, as a result, breakthroughs in this field are likely to have a significant impact on the future of technology.

Contents

1 History
2 Fundamentals
3 Materials in industry
   3.1 Ceramics and glasses
   3.2 Composite materials
   3.3 Polymers
   3.4 Metal alloys
4 Sub-disciplines of materials science

    4.1 Methods, processes, and related topics
5 See also
6 References
    6.1 Citations
    6.2 Bibliography
7 Further reading
8 External links
    8.1 Professional organizations
    8.2 International conferences

History

The material of choice of a given era is often a defining point. Phrases such as Stone Age, Bronze Age, Iron Age, and Steel Age are great examples. Originally deriving from the manufacture of ceramics and its putative derivative metallurgy, materials science is one of the oldest forms of engineering and applied science. Modern materials science evolved directly from metallurgy, which itself evolved from mining and (likely) ceramics and the use of fire. A major breakthrough in the understanding of materials occurred in the late 19th century, when the American scientist Josiah Willard Gibbs demonstrated that the thermodynamic properties related to atomic structure in various phases are related to the physical properties of a material. Important elements of modern materials science are a product of the space race: the understanding and engineering of the metallic alloys, and silica and carbon materials, used in the construction of space vehicles enabling the exploration of space. Materials science has driven, and been driven by, the development of revolutionary technologies such as plastics, semiconductors, and biomaterials.

Before the 1960s (and in some cases decades after), many materials science departments were named metallurgy departments, reflecting the 19th and early 20th century emphasis on metals. The field has since broadened to include every class of materials, including ceramics, polymers, semiconductors, magnetic materials, medical implant materials, biological materials and nanomaterials (materiomics).

Fundamentals

The basis of materials science involves relating the desired properties and relative performance of a material in a certain application to the structure of the atoms and phases in that material through characterization. The major determinants of the structure of a material and thus of its properties are its constituent chemical elements and the way in which it has been processed into its final form. These characteristics, taken together and related through the laws of thermodynamics, govern a material's microstructure, and thus its properties.

The manufacture of a perfect crystal of a material is physically impossible. Instead materials scientists manipulate the defects in crystalline materials such as precipitates, grain boundaries (Hall-Petch relationship), interstitial atoms, vacancies or substitutional atoms, to create materials with the desired properties.

Not all materials have a regular crystal structure. Polymers display varying degrees of crystallinity, and many are completely non-crystalline. Glass as, some ceramics, and many natural materials are amorphous, not possessing any long-range order in their atomic arrangements. The study of polymers combines elements of chemical and statistical thermodynamics to give thermodynamic, as well as mechanical, descriptions of physical properties.

In addition to industrial interest, materials science has gradually developed into a field which provides tests for condensed matter or solid state theories. New physics emerge because of the diverse new material properties that need to be explained.

Materials in industry

Radical materials advances can drive the creation of new products or even new industries, but stable industries also employ materials scientists to make incremental improvements and troubleshoot issues with currently used materials. Industrial applications of materials science include materials design, cost-benefit tradeoffs in industrial production of materials, processing techniques (casting, rolling, welding, ion implantation, crystal growth, thin-film deposition, sintering, glassblowing, etc.), and analytical techniques (characterization techniques such as electron microscopy, X-ray diffraction, calorimetry, nuclear microscopy

(HEFIB), Rutherford backscattering, neutron diffraction, small-angle X-ray scattering (SAXS), etc.).

Besides material characterization, the material scientist/engineer also deals with the extraction of materials and their conversion into useful forms. Thus ingot casting, foundry techniques, blast furnace extraction, and electrolytic extraction are all part of the required knowledge of a metallurgist/engineer. Often the presence, absence or variation of minute quantities of secondary elements and compounds in a bulk material will have a great impact on the final properties of the materials produced, for instance, steels are classified based on 1/10 and 1/100 weight percentages of the carbon and other alloying elements they contain. Thus, the extraction and purification techniques employed in the extraction of iron in the blast furnace will have an impact of the quality of steel that may be produced.

The overlap between physics and materials science has led to the offshoot field of materials physics, which is concerned with the physical properties of materials. The approach is generally more macroscopic and applied than in condensed matter physics. See important publications in materials physics for more details on this field of study.

Ceramics and glasses

Another application of the material sciences is the structures of glass and ceramics, typically associated with the most brittle materials. Bonding in ceramics and glasses use covalent and ionic-covalent types with SiO_2 (silica or sand) as a fundamental building block. Ceramics are as soft as clay and as hard as stone and concrete. Usually, they are crystalline in form. Most glasses contain a metal oxide fused with silica. At high temperatures used to prepare glass, the material is a viscous liquid. The structure of glass forms into an amorphous state upon cooling. Windowpanes and eyeglasses are important examples. Fibers of glass are also available. Scratch resistant Corning Gorilla Glass is a well-known example of the application of materials science to drastically improve the properties of common components. Diamond and carbon in its graphite form are considered to be ceramics.

Engineering ceramics are known for their stiffness and stability under high temperatures, compression and electrical stress. Alumina, silicon carbide, and tungsten carbide are made from a fine powder of their constituents in a process of sintering with a binder. Hot pressing provides higher density material. Chemical vapor deposition can place a film of a ceramic on another material. Cermets are ceramic particles containing some metals. The wear resistance of tools is derived from cemented carbides with the metal phase of cobalt and nickel typically added to modify properties.

Composite materials

Filaments are commonly used for reinforcement in composite materials.

Another application of material science in industry is the making of composite materials. Composite materials are structured materials composed of two or more macroscopic phases. Applications range from structural elements such as steel-reinforced concrete, to the thermally insulative tiles which play a key and integral role in NASA's Space Shuttle thermal protection system which is used to protect the surface of the shuttle from the heat of re-entry into the Earth's atmosphere. One example is reinforced Carbon-Carbon (RCC), the light gray material which withstands re-entry temperatures up to 1 510 °C (2 750 °F) and protects the Space Shuttle's wing leading edges and nose cap. RCC is a laminated composite material made from graphite rayon cloth and impregnated with a phenolic resin. After curing at high temperature in an autoclave, the laminate is pyrolized to convert the resin to carbon, impregnated with furfural alcohol in a vacuum chamber, and cured/pyrolized to convert the furfural alcohol to carbon. In order to provide oxidation resistance for reuse capability, the outer layers of the RCC are converted to silicon carbide.

Other examples can be seen in the "plastic" casings of television sets, cellphones and so on. These plastic casings are usually a composite material made up of a thermoplastic matrix such as acrylonitrile-butadiene-styrene (ABS) in which calcium carbonate chalk, talc, glass fibers or carbon fibers have been added for added strength, bulk, or electrostatic dispersion. These additions may be referred to as reinforcing fibers, or dispersants, depending on their purpose.

Polymers

Polymers are also an important part of materials science. Polymers are the raw materials (the resins) used to make what we commonly call plastics. Plastics are really the final product, created after one or more polymers or additives have been added to a resin during processing, which is then shaped into a final form. Polymers which have been around, and which are in current widespread use, include polyethylene, polypropylene, PVC, polystyrene, nylons, polyesters, acrylics, polyurethanes, and polycarbonates. Plastics are generally classified as "commodity", "specialty" and "engineering" plastics.

PVC (polyvinyl-chloride) is widely used, inexpensive, and annual production quantities are large. It lends itself to an incredible array of applications, from artificial leather to electrical insulation and cabling, packaging and containers. Its fabrication and processing are simple and well-established. The versatility of PVC is due to the wide range of plasticisers and other additives that it accepts. The term "additives" in polymer science refers to the chemicals and compounds added to the polymer base to modify its material properties.

Polycarbonate would be normally considered an engineering plastic (other examples include PEEK, ABS). Engineering plastics are valued for their superior strengths and other special material properties. They are usually not used for disposable applications, unlike commodity plastics.

Specialty plastics are materials with unique characteristics, such as ultra-high strength, electrical conductivity, electro-fluorescence, high thermal stability, etc.

The dividing lines between the various types of plastics is not based on material but rather on their properties and applications. For instance, polyethylene (PE) is a cheap, low friction polymer commonly used to make disposable shopping bags and trash bags, and is considered a commodity plastic, whereas medium-density polyethylene (MDPE) is used for underground gas and water pipes, and another variety called Ultra-high Molecular Weight Polyethylene UHMWPE is an engineering plastic which is used extensively as the glide rails for industrial equipment and the low-friction socket in implanted hip joints.

Metal alloys

The study of metal alloys is a significant part of materials science. Of all the metallic alloys in use today, the alloys of iron (steel, stainless steel, cast iron, tool steel, alloy steels) make up the largest proportion both by quantity and commercial value. Iron alloyed with various proportions of carbon gives low, mid and high carbon steels. An iron carbon alloy is only considered steel if the carbon level is between 0.01% and 2.00%. For the steels, the hardness and tensile strength of the steel is related to the amount of carbon present, with increasing carbon levels also leading to lower ductility and toughness. Heat treatment processes such as quenching and tempering can significantly change these properties however. Cast Iron is defined as an iron-carbon alloy with more than 2.00% but less than 6.67% carbon. Stainless steel is defined as a regular steel alloy with greater than 10% by weight alloying content of Chromium. Nickel and Molybdenum are typically also found in stainless steels.

Other significant metallic alloys are those of aluminium, titanium, copper and magnesium. Copper alloys have been known for a long time (since the Bronze Age), while the alloys of the other three metals have been relatively recently developed. Due to the chemical reactivity of these metals, the electrolytic extraction processes required were only developed relatively recently. The alloys of aluminium, titanium and magnesium are also known and valued for their high strength-to-weight ratios and, in the case of magnesium, their ability to provide electromagnetic shielding. These materials are ideal for situations where high strength-to-weight ratios are more important than bulk cost, such as in the aerospace industry and certain automotive engineering applications.

Sub-disciplines of materials science

Below is a list of disciplines within or related to the materials science field. These range from biomaterials, to ceramics, to metals, to textile reinforced materials. Also note that these are linked to the respective main article.

Biomaterials-materials that are derived from and/or used with life forms.

Ceramography-the study of the microstructures of high-temperature materials and refractories, including structural ceramics such as RCC, polycrystalline silicon carbide and transformation toughened ceramics.

Crystallography-the study of regular arrangement of atoms and ions in a solid, the defects associated with crystal structures such as grain boundaries and dislocations, and the characterization of these structures and their relation to physical properties.

Electronic and magnetic materials-materials such as semiconductors used to create integrated circuits, storage media, sensors, and other devices.

Forensic engineering-the study of how products fail, and the vital role of the materials of construction.

Forensic materials engineering-the study of material failure, and the light it sheds on how engineers specify materials in their product.

Glass science-any non-crystalline material including inorganic glasses, vitreous metals and non-oxide glasses.

Materials characterization-such as diffraction with X-rays, electrons, or neutrons, and various forms of spectroscopy and chemical analysis such as Raman spectroscopy, energy-dispersive spectroscopy (EDS), chromatography, thermal analysis, electron microscope analysis, etc., in order to understand and define the properties of materials. See also List of surface analysis methods.

Metallography-Metallography is the study of the physical structure and components of metals, typically using microscopy.

Metallurgy-the study of metals and their alloys, including their extraction, microstructure and processing.

Microtechnology-study of materials and processes and their interaction, allowing microfabrication of structures of micrometric dimensions, such as Microelectromechanical systems (MEMS).

Nanotechnology-rigorously, the study of materials where the effects of quantum confinement, the Gibbs-Thomson effect, or any other effect only present at the nanoscale is the defining property of the material; but more commonly, it is the creation and study of materials whose defining structural properties are anywhere from less than a nanometer to one hundred nanometers in scale, such as molecularly engineered materials.

Rheology-Some practitioners consider rheology a sub-field of materials science, because it can cover any material that flows. However, modern rheology typically deals with non-Newtonian fluid dynamics, so it is often considered a sub-field of continuum mechanics. See also granular material.

Surface science/catalysis-interactions and structures between solid-gas solid-liquid or solid-solid interfaces.

Textile reinforced materials-materials in the form of ceramic or concrete are reinforced with a primarily woven or non-woven textile structure to impose high strength with comparatively more flexibility to withstand vibrations and sudden jerks.

Tribology-the study of the wear of materials due to friction and other factors.

Methods, processes, and related topics[edit]

Below are links to topics that explain methods, processes and related topics in order to enhance understanding of materials science.

Alloying, corrosion, and thermal or mechanical processing, for a specialized treatment of metallurgical materials-with applications ranging from aerospace and industrial equipment to the civil industries.

Biomaterials, physiology, biomechanics, biochemistry, for a specialized understanding of how materials integrate into biological systems, e.g., through materiomics.

Crystallography, quantum chemistry or quantum physics, for the structure (symmetry and defects) and bonding in materials (e.g., ionic, metallic, covalent, and van der Waals bonding).

Diffraction and wave mechanics, for the science behind characterization systems, e.g., X-ray diffraction (XRD) transmission electron microscopy (TEM)

Electronic properties of materials, and solid-state physics, for the understanding of the electronic, thermal, magnetic, and optical properties of materials

Mechanical behavior of materials, to understand the mechanical properties of materials, defects and their propagation, and their behavior under static, dynamic, and cyclic loads.

Phase transformation kinetics, for the kinetics of phase transformations (with particular emphasis on solid-solid phase transitions).

Polymer properties, synthesis, and characterization, for a specialized understanding of how polymers behave, how they are made, and how they are characterized; exciting applications of polymers include liquid crystal displays (LCDs, the displays found in most cell phones, cameras, and iPods), novel photovoltaic devices based on semiconductor polymers (which, unlike the traditional silicon solar panels, are flexible and cheap to manufacture, albeit with lower efficiency), and membranes for room-temperature fuel cells (as proton exchange membranes) and filtration systems in the environmental and biomedical fields.

Semiconductor materials and semiconductor devices, for a specialized understanding of the advanced processes used in industry (e.g. crystal growth techniques, thin-film deposition, ion implantation, photolithography), their properties, and their integration in electronic devices.

Solid-state physics is the study of rigid matter, or solids, through methods such as quantum mechanics, crystallography, electromagnetism, and metallurgy. It is the largest branch of condensed matter physics. Solid-state physics studies how the large-scale properties of solid materials result from their atomic-scale properties. Thus, solid-state physics forms the theoretical basis of materials science. It also has direct applications, for example in the technology of transistors and semiconductors.

Thermodynamics, statistical mechanics to describe the thermodynamics of materials.

Physical chemistry is the study of the physics of chemical systems.

Phase equilibrium conditions, phase diagrams of materials systems (multiphase, multi-component, reacting and non-reacting systems).